THE DISRUPTER SERIES: DIGITAL CURRENCY AND BLOCKCHAIN TECHNOLOGY

HEARING

BEFORE THE

SUBCOMMITTEE ON COMMERCE, MANUFACTURING, AND TRADE

OF THE

COMMITTEE ON ENERGY AND COMMERCE

HOUSE OF REPRESENTATIVES

ONE HUNDRED FOURTEENTH CONGRESS

SECOND SESSION

MARCH 16, 2016

Serial No. 114–126

Printed for the use of the Committee on Energy and Commerce

energycommerce.house.gov

U.S. GOVERNMENT PUBLISHING OFFICE

20–322 PDF   WASHINGTON : 2016

For sale by the Superintendent of Documents, U.S. Government Publishing Office
Internet: bookstore.gpo.gov   Phone: toll free (866) 512–1800; DC area (202) 512–1800
Fax: (202) 512–2104   Mail: Stop IDCC, Washington, DC 20402–0001

COMMITTEE ON ENERGY AND COMMERCE

FRED UPTON, Michigan
Chairman

JOE BARTON, Texas
  Chairman Emeritus
ED WHITFIELD, Kentucky
JOHN SHIMKUS, Illinois
JOSEPH R. PITTS, Pennsylvania
GREG WALDEN, Oregon
TIM MURPHY, Pennsylvania
MICHAEL C. BURGESS, Texas
MARSHA BLACKBURN, Tennessee
  Vice Chairman
STEVE SCALISE, Louisiana
ROBERT E. LATTA, Ohio
CATHY McMORRIS RODGERS, Washington
GREGG HARPER, Mississippi
LEONARD LANCE, New Jersey
BRETT GUTHRIE, Kentucky
PETE OLSON, Texas
DAVID B. McKINLEY, West Virginia
MIKE POMPEO, Kansas
ADAM KINZINGER, Illinois
H. MORGAN GRIFFITH, Virginia
GUS M. BILIRAKIS, Florida
BILL JOHNSON, Ohio
BILLY LONG, Missouri
RENEE L. ELLMERS, North Carolina
LARRY BUCSHON, Indiana
BILL FLORES, Texas
SUSAN W. BROOKS, Indiana
MARKWAYNE MULLIN, Oklahoma
RICHARD HUDSON, North Carolina
CHRIS COLLINS, New York
KEVIN CRAMER, North Dakota

FRANK PALLONE, JR., New Jersey
  Ranking Member
BOBBY L. RUSH, Illinois
ANNA G. ESHOO, California
ELIOT L. ENGEL, New York
GENE GREEN, Texas
DIANA DeGETTE, Colorado
LOIS CAPPS, California
MICHAEL F. DOYLE, Pennsylvania
JANICE D. SCHAKOWSKY, Illinois
G.K. BUTTERFIELD, North Carolina
DORIS O. MATSUI, California
KATHY CASTOR, Florida
JOHN P. SARBANES, Maryland
JERRY McNERNEY, California
PETER WELCH, Vermont
BEN RAY LUJAN, New Mexico
PAUL TONKO, New York
JOHN A. YARMUTH, Kentucky
YVETTE D. CLARKE, New York
DAVID LOEBSACK, Iowa
KURT SCHRADER, Oregon
JOSEPH P. KENNEDY, III, Massachusetts
TONY CARDENAS, California

————

SUBCOMMITTEE ON COMMERCE, MANUFACTURING, AND TRADE

MICHAEL C. BURGESS, Texas
Chairman

LEONARD LANCE, New Jersey
  Vice Chairman
MARSHA BLACKBURN, Tennessee
GREGG HARPER, Mississippi
BRETT GUTHRIE, Kentucky
PETE OLSON, Texas
MIKE POMPEO, Kansas
ADAM KINZINGER, Illinois
GUS M. BILIRAKIS, Florida
SUSAN W. BROOKS, Indiana
MARKWAYNE MULLIN, Oklahoma
FRED UPTON, Michigan *(ex officio)*

JANICE D. SCHAKOWSKY, Illinois
  Ranking Member
YVETTE D. CLARKE, New York
JOSEPH P. KENNEDY, III, Massachusetts
TONY CARDENAS, California
BOBBY L. RUSH, Illinois
G.K. BUTTERFIELD, North Carolina
PETER WELCH, Vermont
FRANK PALLONE, JR., New Jersey *(ex officio)*

(II)

CONTENTS

THE DISRUPTER SERIES: DIGITAL CURRENCY AND BLOCKCHAIN TECHNOLOGY

WEDNESDAY, MARCH 16, 2016

HOUSE OF REPRESENTATIVES,
SUBCOMMITTEE ON COMMERCE, MANUFACTURING, AND
TRADE,
COMMITTEE ON ENERGY AND COMMERCE,
Washington, DC.

The subcommittee met, pursuant to call, at 11:50 a.m., in room 2123 Rayburn House Office Building, Hon. Michael C. Burgess (chairman of the subcommittee) presiding.

Members present: Representatives Burgess, Lance, Bilirakis, Brooks, Schakowsky, Cárdenas, and Pallone (ex officio).

Staff present: Leighton Brown, Deputy Press Secretary; James Decker, Policy Coordinator, Commerce, Manufacturing, and Trade; Graham Dufault, Counsel, Commerce, Manufacturing, and Trade; Melissa Froelich, Counsel, Commerce, Manufacturing, and Trade; Giulia Giannangeli, Legislative Clerk; Paul Nagle, Chief Counsel, Commerce, Manufacturing, and Trade; Olivia Trusty, Professional Staff Member, Commerce, Manufacturing, and Trade; Dylan Vorbach, Deputy Press Secretary; Michelle Ash, Democratic Chief Counsel, Commerce, Manufacturing, and Trade; Christine Brennan, Democratic Press Secretary; Jeff Carroll, Democratic Staff Director; Caroline Paris-Behr, Democratic Policy Analyst; Timothy Robinson, Democratic Chief Counsel; Diana Rudd, Democratic Legal Fellow; and Matt Schumacher, Democratic Press Assistant.

Mr. BURGESS. The Subcommittee on Commerce, Manufacturing, and Trade will now come to order. I will recognize myself 5 minutes for the purposes of an opening statement.

OPENING STATEMENT OF HON. MICHAEL C. BURGESS, A REPRESENTATIVE IN CONGRESS FROM THE STATE OF TEXAS

I want to welcome all of our witnesses. Good morning, and welcome to the next hearing in our Disrupter Series. Today we will be examining digital currency and blockchain technology. This technology has the potential to disrupt a whole host of industries from financial services to manufacturing, supply chain management, and to health care records, by infusing transparency and trust in traditionally closed systems.

This is a new technology. The White Paper describing the first public blockchain application, Bitcoin, was published in 2009, and already there has been a billion dollars in capital investment over 1,000 firms, most of which are startup companies.

(1)

Having seen the development of email, development of the Internet, transitioning of the United States economy to the digital space in the last two-and-a-half decades, I am interested to hear from our panel about what the development of blockchain technology means for the next 25 years of global commerce.

Bitcoin is the best-known digital currency and a good case study for the disruptive nature of the blockchain. The Federal Reserve Bank of Chicago highlighted how Bitcoin's blockchain solves two basic issues with digital currency, by controlling the creation and avoiding its duplication. Bitcoin limits an individual's ability to copy and paste new money files to double spend—we do that in the Federal Government sometimes—to double-spend digital wealth through advanced cryptographic signatures.

The solution Bitcoin presents to currency may also be applied to other asset cases, including intellectual property, mortgages, and other property records. In a way, it provides a way to create singular possession online, mimicking possession in the physical world, but with a transparent and immutable ledger recording of the possession along the way.

While there have been issues through the development and growth of Bitcoin, including some of the Mt. Gox issues, the technology has withstood the stress of growth to date. In the same way that the Internet has transformed communications, the adoption of blockchain technology has the potential to disrupt digital asset transfers.

Cyber security is at the forefront of this subcommittee's activities in this Congress. It is fascinating to see the possibility of another technological revolution on the horizon that could help address the trust and security issues that are a daily challenge for individuals and companies in every sector of the United States economy.

However, to serve as an alternative to today's settlement mechanisms, the technology must demonstrate the scaleability needed to handle the volumes of transactions to flow through United States firms on a daily basis. I do hope our panelists will discuss their work and address the concerns about the viability of the blockchain moving forward.

I have heard about many potential use cases for this technology, including digital health records, where security and immutability are necessities. I would be interested to hear how blockchain technology could help individuals gain control over their health records and transparency into how those records are created and shared.

Today's witnesses represent a variety of interests in digital currency and blockchain technology industries. We will hear about what consumers can do today using digital currency. We will also hear about consumer protection issues that may develop. Even more exciting is the potential for consumer benefits that have yet to be realized for the firms that leverage the blockchain.

Currently, a number of regulatory bodies at the State and Federal level have weighed in or are considering action around Bitcoin and other blockchain applications. While there are serious concerns to be addressed with the anti-money laundering effects for digital currency, we should also be cognizant of the future applications of the blockchain technology that may improve transparency in both the public and private sectors. These future applications could be stifled if the regulatory environment becomes too burdensome on small companies trying to leverage this new technology.

Once again, I want to thank all of our witnesses for taking time to inform and educate us about the applications and future potential of digital currency and blockchain technology. I certainly look forward to a thoughtful and engaging discussion.

[The prepared statement of Mr. Burgess follows:]

PREPARED STATEMENT OF HON. MICHAEL C. BURGESS

Good morning and welcome to the next hearing in our Disrupter Series. Today we will be examining digital currency and blockchain technology. This technology has the potential to disrupt a whole host of industries from financial services to manufacturing supply chain management to health care records by infusing transparency and trust into traditionally closed systems.

This is an incredibly new technology—the whitepaper describing the first public blockchain application, Bitcoin, was published in 2009. And already there has been $1 billion in capital investment to over a thousand firms, most of which are startups.

Having seen the development of email, the Internet, and the transitioning of the U.S.'s economy to the digital space in the last two and a half decades, I am interested to hear from our panel about what the development of blockchain technology means for the next 25 years of global commerce.

Bitcoin is the best known digital currency and as a good case study for the disruptive nature of the blockchain. The Federal Reserve Bank of Chicago highlighted how Bitcoin's blockchain solves the two basic issues with digital currency: controlling its creation and avoiding its duplication. Bitcoin limits individual's ability to copy and paste new "money files" to double spend or accumulate "digital wealth" through advanced cryptographic signatures. The solution Bitcoin presents to currency may also be applied to other asset cases including intellectual property, mortgages, and other property records. In a way—it provides a way to create singular possession online, mimicking possession in the physical world, but with a transparent and immutable ledger recording the possession along the way.

While there have been issues through the development and growth of Bitcoin, including the Mt. Gox issues, the technology has withstood the stress of growth to date. In the same way that the Internet transformed communications, the adoption of Blockchain technology has the potential to disrupt digital asset transfers. Cybersecurity is at the forefront of this subcommittee's activities this Congress. It is fascinating to see the possibility of another technological revolution on the horizon that could help address the trust and security issues that are a daily challenge for individuals and companies in every sector of the US economy.

However, to serve as an alternative to today's settlement mechanisms the technology must demonstrate the scalability needed to handle the volume of transactions that flow through U.S. firms on a daily basis. I hope the panelists will discuss their work to address concerns about the viability of the blockchain moving forward.

I have heard about many potential uses cases for this technology, including for digital health records, where security and immutability are necessities. I would be interested to hear how blockchain technology could help individuals gain control over their health records and transparency into how those records are created and shared.

Today's witnesses represent a variety of interests in digital currency and Blockchain technology industries. We will hear about what consumers can do today using digital currency. We will also hear about consumer protection issues that may develop. Even more exciting is the potential consumer benefits that have yet to be realized for firms that leverage the blockchain.

Currently, a number of regulatory bodies at the State and Federal level have weighed in, or are considering action, around Bitcoin or other blockchain applications. While there are serious concerns to be addressed with anti-money laundering efforts for digital currency, we should also be cognizant of future applications of the blockchain technology that may improve transparency in both the public and private sector. These future applications could be stifled if the regulatory environment becomes too burdensome on small companies trying to leverage this new technology. I thank the witnesses for taking the time to inform us about the applications and future potential of digital currency and blockchain technology. I look forward to a thoughtful and engaging discussion.

Mr. BURGESS. I will yield back my time and recognize Mr. Cárdenas of California as the ranking member of the subcommittee.

OPENING STATEMENT OF HON. TONY CÁRDENAS, A REPRESENTATIVE IN CONGRESS FROM THE STATE OF CALIFORNIA

Mr. CÁRDENAS. Thank you very much, Mr. Chairman. I would like to thank all the witnesses for coming forward today to help enlighten us about your views on what we are going to talk about in this hearing today. In this hearing, we are looking at digital currency and blockchain terms that don't often enter every conversations. Although with today's Metro shutdown, the ride-hailing services using the blockchain may have helped people get here to work today.

As we continue this subcommittee's Disrupter Series, we again run into the same key question—how must yesterday's rules evolve to fit today's technology. Digital currency like Bitcoin lacks many of the features we usually associate with traditional money like the U.S. dollar. It doesn't come in paper bills. It is not issued or guaranteed by a Government. Electronic transactions with digital currency may not require a bank to serve as an intermediary.

Digital currency has not been widely adopted in part because it has several changes. Digital currencies lack some of the protections provided for more traditional financial products. The value of currencies like Bitcoin has fluctuated wildly. Few merchants accept them at this point. Meanwhile, digital currencies have become associated with illegal transactions such as money laundering, ransomware, and the sale of illicit goods and services.

If digital currencies are to be widely accepted at legitimate payments, they need to provide sufficient safeguards for their users, and they need to come under an adequate regulatory regime to address unlawful use, particularly in terms of money laundering and financing of terrorism. But digital currency is really just our entry point for discussion of a more fundamental innovation—blockchain.

Blockchain is this concept of a digital public ledger to track transactions. It is an innovation that can have many different applications. Blockchain could have many other applications beyond digital currency. Proponents talk about blockchain's ability to cut out intermediaries. In some cases, this could be helpful.

At the same time, we need to think about what we may be losing in the process of cutting out this middleman. For example, in financial transactions, the middleman is the bank, and banks have rules and reporting requirements they must follow to prevent money laundering and financing of terrorism. If the bank is cut out, we need alternative means to detect such activity.

While blockchain is theoretically transparent as an open ledger, permissioned blockchain, where the ledger is private or invitation-only, could potentially enable anti-competitive activity. These are not arguments against blockchain. Rather, they are challenges for developers to address as innovation moves forward. Developers have a responsibility to protect user privacy, stop fraud, and prevent use of their products for illegal activity.

Carrying out these responsibilities may look different than it did for earlier products, but let's be clear. Compliance with rules to protect consumers or protect our security is not an inconvenience. It is a necessary part of participating in our economy. One of our roles on the subcommittee is to wrestle with how new technology affects consumers and interests with the law.

States are already figuring out how to regulate these new products and markets. Federal agencies are monitoring digital currency markets. These efforts require understanding the unique attributes of these new technologies. As we start examining this new space, I hope our witnesses can help inform our discussion and provide answers on not only how blockchain can be used but also how these uses interact with rules to protect consumers and protect security.

With that, I welcome our witnesses, and I look forward to the testimony today.

Mr. BURGESS. The Chair thanks the gentleman. The gentleman yields back.

The Chair recognizes the gentleman from New Jersey, Mr. Pallone, 5 minutes for your opening statement, please.

OPENING STATEMENT OF HON. FRANK PALLONE, JR., A REPRESENTATIVE IN CONGRESS FROM THE STATE OF NEW JERSEY

Mr. PALLONE. Thank you, Chairman Burgess. While some members surely have heard of Bitcoin, few have likely heard of the recordkeeping software underpinning it called blockchain. Today we will have the opportunity to explore the benefits and risks of using crypto-currency sometimes referred to as virtual or digital currencies. We also will get an understanding of the benefits and risks of the blockchain for financial and nonfinancial uses.

Whether using Bitcoin, the most well-known and widely used crypto-currency, or another one, peer-to-peer digital transactions have the potential to reduce fees and wait times for consumer purchases. In addition, crypto-currencies can offer advantages to underbanked and unbanked populations, especially in regions where state-backed currency is consistently unstable and traditional financial services are less accessible. They also may offer users increased privacy in comparison to traditional payment methods.

However, at the same time crypto-currencies raise important issues that should be explored, they are not legal tender, and their value is not guaranteed by any central authority. Therefore, they have proven to be vulnerable to price volatility, deflation, and hacking. In addition, many existing consumer protections, such as requirements that banks have systems in place to limit consumer loss and detect money laundering, may not apply to crypto-currencies.

For example, current law ensures that you are not responsible for unauthorized credit card charges over $50. No such protections exist for purchases made with crypto-currency. Also, digital payments can be irreversible, making simple consumer transactions like returns and chargebacks more complicated or impossible.

While originally created for crypto-currency, the recordkeeping technology, blockchain, has gained enormous interest in the last

6

few years with more than \$1 billion raised in venture capital so far. In the financial sector, firms are looking at placing stock and bond trades on the blockchain. In the nonfinancial arena, the full range of possibilities may be endless. Blockchain is being tested for possible applications in health care, green energy, copyright, and voting, to name a few.

The blockchain can automate contracts, making them faster to complete. They can increase transparency in property rights disputes and help protect intellectual property. And, in many sectors, the blockchain may improve privacy protections, reduce human error, and lower administrative costs.

Just as with crypto-currencies, blockchain raises important issues for us to explore. Some experts have pointed out that permission blockchains, in which only vetted and approved users can participate, may use anti-competitive tactics or price-fixing that would violate antitrust regulations. Others have suggested that the blockchain is too rigid for many potential applications. It does not include the necessary flexibilities to ensure consumers have basic rights, such as the ability to resolve disputes.

So I just want to reiterate that consumer protections must be considered as these new technologies are developed. I look forward to hearing from all of our witnesses about the current and future uses of crypto-currencies and the blockchain, and the consumer protections that go with them hand in hand.

And, again, Mr. Chairman, I thank you, and I yield back the balance of my time.

[The prepared statement of Mr. Pallone follows:]

PREPARED STATEMENT OF HON. FRANK PALLONE, JR.

Thank you, Chairman Burgess. While some members surely have heard of Bitcoin, few have likely heard of the recordkeeping software underpinning it called the blockchain.

Today we will have the opportunity to explore the benefits and risks of using cryptocurrencies, sometimes referred to as virtual or digital currencies. We also will get an understanding of the benefits and risks of the blockchain, for financial and nonfinancial uses.

Whether using Bitcoin, the most well-known and widely used cryptocurrency, or another one, peer-to-peer digital transactions have the potential to reduce fees and wait times for consumer purchases. In addition, cryptocurrencies can offer advantages to underbanked and unbanked populations, especially in regions where state-backed currency is consistently unstable and traditional financial services are less accessible. They also may offer users increased privacy in comparison to traditional payment methods.

However, at the same time, cryptocurrencies raise important issues that should be explored. They are not legal tender, and their value is not guaranteed by any central authority. Therefore, they have proven to be vulnerable to price volatility, deflation, and hacking.

In addition, many existing consumer protections, such as requirements that banks have systems in place to limit consumer loss and detect money laundering, may not apply to cryptocurrencies. For example, current law ensures that you are not responsible for unauthorized credit card charges over \$50. No such protections exist for purchases made with cryptocurrency. Also, digital payments can be irreversible, making simple consumer transactions like returns and chargebacks more complicated or impossible.

While originally created for cryptocurrency, the record-keeping technology—blockchain—has gained enormous interest in the last few years, with more than one billion dollars raised in venture capital so far. In the financial sector, firms are looking at placing stock and bond trades on the blockchain. In the nonfinancial arena, the full range of possibilities may be endless—blockchain is being tested for possible applications in health care, green energy, copyright, and voting, to name a few.

The blockchain can automate contracts, making them faster to complete. They can increase transparency in property rights disputes and help protect intellectual property. And in many sectors, the blockchain may improve privacy protections, reduce human error, and lower administrative costs.

Just as with cryptocurrencies, blockchain raises important issues for us to explore. Some experts have pointed out that permissioned blockchains, in which only vetted and approved users can participate, may use anticompetitive tactics or price fixing that would violate antitrust regulations. Others have suggested that the blockchain is too rigid for many potential applications, and does not include the necessary flexibilities to ensure consumers have basic rights such as the ability to resolve disputes.

I want to reiterate that consumer protections must be considered as these new technologies are developed. I look forward to hearing from all of our witnesses about the current and future uses of cryptocurrencies and the blockchain and the consumer protections that go with them, hand-in-hand. Thank you and I yield back.

Mr. BURGESS. The Chair thanks the gentleman. The gentleman yields back.

Seeing no other members present who wish to give an opening statement, the Chair would like to remind members that, pursuant to committee rules, all members' opening statements will be made part of the record.

And, again, we want to thank our witnesses for being here with us this afternoon, for taking their valuable time to testify and educate the subcommittee. Today's witnesses will have the opportunity to summarize their opening statement, followed by a round of questions from members. Our witnesses for today's panel hearing include Mr. Jerry Brito, Executive Director at Coin Center; Mr. Juan Suarez, counsel at Coinbase; Mr. Jerry Cuomo, Vice President of Blockchain Technologies at IBM; Mr. Paul Snow, Chief Architect at Factom; Mr. John Beccia, General Counsel and Chief Compliance Officer at Circle Internet Financial; Mr. Dana Syracuse, former Associate General Counsel of the New York Department of Financial Services at BuckleySandler LLP; and Mr. Matthew Roszak, Chairman of the Chamber of Digital Commerce and co-founder of Bloq, Incorporated.

We certainly appreciate you all being here today. We recognize the significant expertise that is before our panel today. We will begin the panel with you, Mr. Brito, and you are recognized for 5 minutes for an opening statement.

STATEMENTS OF JERRY BRITO, EXECUTIVE DIRECTOR, COIN CENTER; JUAN SUAREZ, COUNSEL, COINBASE, INC.; JERRY CUOMO, VICE PRESIDENT, BLOCKCHAIN TECHNOLOGIES, IBM; PAUL SNOW, CHIEF ARCHITECT AND CO–FOUNDER, FACTOM, INC.; JOHN BECCIA, GENERAL COUNSEL AND CHIEF COMPLIANCE OFFICER, CIRCLE INTERNET FINANCIAL; DANA V. SYRACUSE, COUNSEL, BUCKLEYSANDLER, LLP; AND MATTHEW ROSZAK, CHAIRMAN, CHAMBER OF DIGITAL COMMERCE, AND CO–FOUNDER, BLOQ, INC.

STATEMENT OF JERRY BRITO

Mr. BRITO. Mr. Chairman and Ranking Member, members of the committee, my name is Jerry Brito, and I am the Executive Director of Coin Center, an independent nonprofit research and advocacy center that is focused on the public policy issues facing crypto-currencies like Bitcoin and Ethereum. Our mission is to be a resource to policymakers and members of the media who want to learn   more

about digital currency technology and to develop legal research
that meets the policy challenges this technology presents.

I want to thank you for inviting me to participate in this hearing.
I would like to provide some background on the technology we are
discussing. I would also be happy to answer any technical questions that you might have or to explain some of the regulatory activity that we have seen to date.

Now, digital currencies are nothing new. They have existed for
decades from Microsoft points to Facebook credits to airline miles,
and neither are online payment systems new. PayPal, Visa, Western Union Pay, these are all examples. So what is it about Bitcoin
and similar cryptograph-based currencies that make them unique?
Bitcoin is the world's first completely decentralized digital currency, and it is the decentralized part that makes it unique.

Decentralized means that there is no issuer, no central authority,
and there is no company, no building, no server. Before the invention of Bitcoin, for two parties to transact online, to transact electronically, always required a trusted third party, someone like
PayPal or Bank of America.

Why was that? Well, what would an online transaction have
looked like without a trust intermediary? Let's think first about a
cash transaction where no third party is needed. If I hand you a
$100 bill, you now have it and now I don't, and we can verify that
the transaction has taken place by looking at our hands.

If we try to do that online, what would that look like? Well, we
would have to represent the $100 billion digitally, and we would
have to basically create a $100 digital file, and I would attach that
$100 file to a message, much like I might attach a photo or Word
document to an email, and I would send it to you.

You would then have the $100 file, but what about me? When
I email a Word document to you, is a document deleted from my
computer? No. I retain a perfect digital copy. So if it was a $100
file, I would retain the perfect digital copy of that same $100 bill,
and I could send it to a second person or a third person or a fourth.
This is what computer scientists call the double-spending problem,
and we solve that problem by employing trusted third parties like
PayPal.

When I send you $100 using PayPal, I don't communicate di-
rectly with you. Instead, I ask PayPal to deduct that amount from
my balance on their ledger and add it to yours. This means, however, that we must each have an account with the same party that
we trust. Bitcoin's invention is revolutionary, because for the first
time the double-spending problem can be solved without the need
for a third party. Bitcoin does this by distributing the necessary
ledger among all the users of the system, via a peer-to-peer network.

Every transaction that occurs in the Bitcoin network is registered in a distributed public ledger which is called the blockchain.
The global peer-to-peer network, composed of thousands of peers,
takes the place of the intermediary. You and I can now transact
online without an intermediary.

Now, why would one use Bitcoin instead of a traditional payment
system? There are many reasons, but chief among them is because
if there is no intermediary transaction costs can be lower, making

Bitcoin transactions cheaper and faster than some existing sys-tems. And perhaps more importantly, though, Bitcoin allows for new kinds of transactions that were never before feasible, including micro transactions, self-executing contracts, and other innovations. Bitcoin is an open network protocol. This means that unlike PayPal or a credit card network, you don't need permission to join and transact. As a result, Bitcoin is an open platform for innovation, just like the Internet itself. In fact, Bitcoin looks today very much like the Internet did in 1995.

So some dismissed the Internet then as a curiosity, but many could see that such an open platform for innovation would allow for world-changing applications to be built on top of it. Few in 1995 could have foreseen Facebook or Skype or Netflix, but they could see that all the building blocks were there for some amazing innovations. Bitcoin is like that today. We can't conceive yet what will be the killer applications on Bitcoin and open crypto-currencies, but it is pretty obvious the day will come.

Bitcoin faces some challenges, however, and chief among them is regulatory uncertainty, especially at the State level. If we think back again to the early Internet, it was not until the Government made it clear that it would pursue a light-touch regulatory approach that Internet innovation really took off.

Bitcoin today is in need of similar commitment from Government. Therefore, as you consider regulatory policies that affect this infant technology, you should take care to measure their impact on continued innovation. If you need any further assistance as you consider digital currencies, please do not hesitate to contact us at Coin Center. Again, our mission is to build a better understanding of these technologies and to promote a regulatory climate that preserves the freedom to innovate using blockchain technologies. We are more than happy to connect you with the appropriate academics, experts, and practitioners in the space.

Thank you for your time, and I look forward to your questions.

[The prepared statement of Mr. Brito follows:]

Testimony of

Jerry Brito
Executive Director
Coin Center

Before the

Subcommittee on Commerce, Manufacturing & Trade
Committee on Energy & Commerce
U.S. House of Representatives

Hearing on

Digital Currency and Blockchain Technology

March 16, 2016

Mr. Chairman and members of the committee:

My name is Jerry Brito and I am the Executive Director of Coin Center, a non-profit research and advocacy center focused on the public policy issues facing cryptocurrencies like Bitcoin. I applaud you for taking the time to learn more about this technology and its social, economic, and policy implications. In what follows, I will provide some background on the technology and touch on its potential benefits and the challenges it poses.

Bitcoin is frequently described as a "digital currency." While that description is accurate, it can be misleading because it is at once too broad and too narrow. It is too broad because Bitcoin is a very particular kind of digital currency—a cryptography based currency (indeed, it is the first of its kind). It is too narrow because although currency is one aspect of the Bitcoin system; Bitcoin is more broadly an Internet protocol with many applications beyond payments or money transfer. Think of it like email or the Web—an open network to which anyone can connect without requiring permission from a central authority, anyone can send a message to anyone else, and on top of which you can freely build many different kinds of applications.

That said, online virtual currencies are nothing new. They have existed for decades. From Microsoft Points to Facebook Credits. Neither are online payments systems new. PayPal, Visa, and Western Union Pay are all examples. So what is it about Bitcoin, and similar cryptography based currencies, that make them unique?

Bitcoin is the world's first completely decentralized digital currency, and it is the "decentralized" part that makes it unique. Prior to Bitcoin's invention in 2009, online currencies or payments systems had to be managed by a central authority. For example, Facebook issuing Facebook Points, or PayPal ensuring that transactions between its customers are reconciled. However, by solving a longstanding conundrum in computer science known as the "double spending" problem, Bitcoin for the first time makes possible transactions online that are person to person, without the need for an intermediary between them, just like cash.

Before the invention of Bitcoin, for two parties to transact electronically always required that they employ a third-party intermediary like PayPal or Visa. Without such intermediaries, there was no way to ensure that money could not be spent twice. To understand why, it is useful to consider cash transactions.

A physical cash transaction requires no intermediary. If I hand you $100 bill, you now have it and I do not. I cannot spend the same $100 bill again because you now have it, and we can verify that you are the sole possessor of the bill simply by looking at our hands. Replicating such a cash-like transaction electronically, however, had been difficult.

If instead of a $100 bill we use a $100 digital file, I can send it to you by attaching it to a message. But as anyone who has ever sent an email attachment knows, when you send a Word document or a photo to a friend, the file is not deleted from your computer; you retain a perfect digital copy. So, if I send you a $100 file, you have no way of verifying that you are now the sole possessor of that file. The same file remains on my computer, and I could send it to a second person. I could spend the same $100 a second and a third time.

The way we solved this conundrum, which computer scientists called the "double-spending problem,"[1] was by employing trusted third-party intermediaries. For example, you and I might have accounts with PayPal, which keeps a ledger of all accountholder balances. To send you $100, I instruct PayPal to make the transfer, and it deducts the amount from my balance and adds it to yours. That transaction reconciles to zero, and at the end of the day all transactions across all accountholders also reconcile to zero. We each trust PayPal to verify balances and transactions using a centralized ledger that it controls.

---

[1] David Chaum, "Achieving Electronic Privacy," *Scientific American* (August 1992): 96–101.

Bitcoin's innovation–and it is a profound one–is that for the first time it solved the double-spending problem without relying on a trusted third-party. Bitcoin accomplishes this feat by distributing the necessary ledger among all users of the system via a peer-to-peer network. Every transaction in the Bitcoin economy is registered in a public ledger called the *blockchain*. Complete copies of the blockchain reside on the computers of everyone who uses Bitcoin. New transactions are checked against the blockchain to ensure that the same Bitcoins have not been previously allocated, thus eliminating the double-spending problem.

Transactions are checked and added to the blockchain by users called "miners," who lend their computers' processing power for that purpose. Miners essentially solve the difficult cryptographic math problems that allow them to securely add transactions to the ledger, and they are awarded newly created Bitcoins for their trouble.[2] This is how new bitcoins are injected into the money supply. As more users become miners and the processing power that is dedicated to mining increases, the Bitcoin protocol also increases the difficulty of the cryptographic problem miners must solve, thus ensuring that new bitcoins are always mined at a predictable and limited rate.

This inflation will not continue forever. Bitcoin was designed to mimic the extraction of gold or other precious metals from the earth–only a limited, known number of the coins can ever be dug up. The arbitrary number chosen to be the cap is 21 million bitcoins. Miners also have a second stream of income: voluntary fees that one can attach to a transaction to ensure that it is promptly processed. Once all bitcoins have been issued, these fees will incentivize miners to continue to process payments. These fees will be set at a market rate based on supply and demand.

This certainty and predictability appeals to many because it makes artificial currency inflation impossible. In most countries, a central bank controls the money supply, and sometimes (such as an economic crisis) it may decide to inject more money into an economy. A central bank does this essentially by printing more money. More cash in the system, however, means that the cash you already hold will be worth less. By contrast, because Bitcoin has no central authority, no one can decide to increase the money supply. The rate of new Bitcoins introduced to the system is based on a public algorithm and is therefore perfectly predictable.

Yet as interesting as Bitcoin's deflationary nature is, it is the decentralized design that makes the innovation truly revolutionary. It means that you and I can transact online without PayPal or any other central authority between us, just as we would if we met in person and exchanged dollar bills. Real digital cash is now possible.

Benefits

---

[2] Peter Van Valkenburgh, What is Bitcoin Mining, and Why is it Necessary? A Backgrounder for Policymakers, Coin Center, Dec. 15, 2014, *available at* https://coincenter.org/2014/12/bitcoin-mining/

You may be thinking to yourself at this point, this is all very interesting, but why would I use Bitcoin when my credit cards work just fine and there is an extensive payments infrastructure in place?

The first answer is that most people in the world do not have access to credit cards or electronic payments, yet they soon will have access to the Internet via smartphones and other inexpensive devices. Bitcoin allows anyone with access to the Internet to engage in mobile commerce even if PayPal or Visa do not serve their country. This is a boon not just to the billions of unbanked persons in the developing world, but also to merchants in the developed world who can now trade with previously untapped markets.

One online technology retailer that accepts bitcoin payments reported that it now sells to nearly 40 countries, many of which are "high-risk markets" to which they previously would not have had access.[3] Customers from India and Pakistan, for example, now have a way of placing an order from a U.S. merchant, and because Bitcoin payments are not reversible, the merchant can be sure he has the money before he ships the goods.

There are many other potential benefits of the technology. For example, micropayments of a few pennies or less are not economically feasible using our existing payments networks. Cryptocurrency technology has the potential to make such tiny payments possible and allow users for the first time to pay directly for the content they consume on websites rather than view ads. Instead of all-you-can-eat plans, digital metering could become a new option for consumers—for minutes of music listened to or video watched or every kilobyte of Wi-Fi used. Additionally, cryptocurrencies make standardized machine-to-machine payments truly feasible for the first time, which will be a key component of the growing "Internet of Things." Imagine being in a hurry and the self-driving Uber car you are riding can pay other autonomous vehicles on the road to let it pass.

Other more prosaic use cases involve settlement of different kinds. For example, international wire transfers today can take days. If the banks at the endpoints of a transfer do not have accounts with each other, they will use one or more intermediary correspondent banks at which they each do have accounts, adding to the cost and time of a transfer. A global ledger used by all banks could make correspondent banking much more efficient. The same principle can be applied to securities and commodities trading by using the ledger to track particular assets rather than simply money.[4]

To date, bitcoins have represented money at a floating exchange rate, and the Bitcoin network has been employed as a fast and inexpensive payments or money transfer system. But there is no reason why particular bitcoins could not represent something besides money. If we conceive of bitcoins simply as tokens, then other applications

---

[3] Dylan Love, "A Guy Who Owns a Bitcoin-Only Electronics Store Is Revealing Everything on Reddit," *Business Insider*, March 18, 2014, http:// www.businessinsider.com/e-commerce-with-bitcoin-2014-3

[4] Brock Cusick, What are Colored Coins? A Backgrounder for Policymakers, Coin Center, Nov. 30, 2014, *available at* https://coincenter.org/2014/11/colored-coins/

become apparent. For example, we could agree that a particular bitcoin (or, indeed, an infinitesimally small fraction of a bitcoin so as to allow for many tokens) represents a house, a car, a share of stock, a futures contract, or an ounce of gold. Conceived of in this way, the Bitcoin blockchain then becomes more than just a payment system. It can be a completely decentralized and perfectly reconciled property registry.

Remittances also help illustrate the potential cost advantages of cryptocurrencies like Bitcoin. In 2012, immigrants to developed countries sent about $400 billion in remittances back to relatives living in developing countries, and that figure is projected to increase to over $500 billion by 2015.[5] According to the World Bank, the global average fee for sending remittances in 2013 was nine percent.[6] With Bitcoin it could be as low as one percent. Remittances can also take days to clear. Bitcoin transactions, on the other hand, are instantaneous, and can take less than an hour to completely confirm.

Finally, Bitcoin is censorship-resistant. For example, after WikiLeaks began releasing its trove of State Department cables, individuals who sought to make a donation to the organization found that many payment processors, including Visa, MasterCard, and PayPal, would not remit money to WikiLeaks due to U.S. government pressure. PayPal even froze the group's account so that it could not access funds it had already collected. Today, WikiLeaks accepts bitcoins for donations, and because Bitcoin is decentralized, there is no intermediary that can be pressured or censored. While this makes prior restraint of financial transactions impossible, it does not preclude a person from being punished after the fact for engaging in illegal transactions.

Unlike cash, Bitcoin is not anonymous, since a public record is made of every transaction.[7] But it is more private than traditional electronic payments, such as credit card transactions, because users' identities need not be tied to the transactions. That said, security researchers have begun to develop techniques to unmask the identities of the persons behind transactions by analyzing the patterns of activity in the block chain, and law enforcement has begun to adopt such techniques.[8]

Challenges

This last benefit of Bitcoin is also the key challenge that it poses to regulators. One person's censorship-resistance is another's money laundering. To date the U.S.

---

[5] World Bank, *Developing Countries to Receive Over $410 Billion in Remittances in 2013, Says World Bank*, Oct. 2, 2013, *available at* http://www.worldbank.org/en/news/press-release/2013/10/02/developing-countries-remittances-2013-world-bank

[6] *Id.*

[7] Adam Ludwin, How Anonymous is Bitcoin? A Backgrounder for Policymakers, Coin Center, Jan. 20, 2015, *available at* https://coincenter.org/2015/01/anonymous-bitcoin/

[8] Jason Weinstein, How Can Law Enforcement Leverage the Blockchain in Investigations? A Backgrounder for Policymakers, Coin Center, May 12, 2015, *available at* https://coincenter.org/2015/05/how-can-law-enforcement-leverage-the-blockchain-in-investigations/

government has reacted to Bitcoin even-handedly, seeking to address its potential misuse while preserving its potential benefits for society and the economy.

The Treasury Department's Financial Crimes Enforcement Network (FinCEN) has found that companies in the business of transmitting value over the Bitcoin network, or exchanging dollars for Bitcoins, must register as money transmitters and comply with Bank Secrecy Act regulations, including requirements to identify customers and file suspicious activity reports.[9] Federal law enforcement has also targeted illegal transactions that employ Bitcoin. The FBI shut down Silk Road, an encrypted website that has facilitated the sale of drugs and other illicit goods, and has targeted other such marketplaces. The SEC has shuttered ponzi schemes in which victims are asked to invest using bitcoins, and the FTC has taken on fraud in the bitcoin mining hardware industry.

While Bitcoin no doubt presents some new challenges to law enforcement, the message from the government has been that it is well positioned to adapt. As Edward Lowery, a special agent with the Secret Service noted at the first Senate hearing on virtual currencies that, "High level international cybercriminals have not by-and-large gravitated to the peer-to-peer cryptocurrency, such as bitcoin."[10] At the same hearing, FinCEN director Jennifer Shasky Calvery said that "Cash is probably still the best medium for laundering money."[11] This was reiterated by David S. Cohen, Treasury's undersecretary for terrorism and financial intelligence, in a speech when he said, "Terrorists generally need 'real' currency, not virtual currency, to pay their expenses -- such as salaries, bribes, weapons, travel, and safe houses. The same is true for those seeking to evade sanctions."[12]

Like email or the web, Bitcoin is an open Internet protocol. This means that anyone can plug into the network and easily transact with anyone else in the world. This creates new opportunities for people who previously did not have access to financial markets, and it also opens up a new world of beneficial permissionless innovation. It also means, however, that criminals can use the open network for illicit purposes–just as criminals use email today. We obviously do not criminalize email, however, because we recognize that its benefits outweigh its risks, and the same is true for cryptocurrencies like Bitcoin.

---

[9] US Department of the Treasury, Financial Crimes and Enforcement Network, "Application of FinCEN's Regulations to Persons Administering, Exchanging, or Using Virtual Currencies" (Guidance FIN-2013-G001, March 18, 2013), *available at* http://fincen.gov/statutes_regs/guidance/html/FIN-2013-G001.html.

[10] Katherine Mangu-Ward, Are Bitcoins Making Money Laundering Easier? Bitcoins are sexy, but cash is still king, *Slate*, Feb. 5, 2014, at http://www.slate.com/articles/technology/future_tense/2014/02/bitcoin_money_laundering_allegations_cash_is_still_king.html

[11] *Id.*

[12] US Department of Treasury, Remarks From Under Secretary of Terrorism and Financial Intelligence David S. Cohen on "Addressing the Illicit Finance Risks of Virtual Currency," March 18, 2014, *available at* https://www.treasury.gov/press-center/press-releases/Pages/jl236.aspx

Consumer protection is another area where regulators are currently focusing their attention. States have begun to look at how digital currencies, such as Bitcoin, and the businesses that utilize them to provide consumer products and services, interact with money transmission and consumer protection policy. Texas and Kansas, for example, have published guidance explaining that third-party bitcoin exchanges *do* engage in money transmission and therefore must be licensed as money transmitters with state authorities. New York, by contrast, has decided to place digital currency businesses under a separate regulatory regime from traditional money transfer and has crafted a so-called, "BitLicense."

In its policy statement on state virtual currency regulation, the Conference of State Bank Supervisors has clearly set out the normative case for consumer protection regulation of digital currencies:

> [M]any virtual currency services are clearly focused on consumer financial services. Such virtual currency service providers are in a position of trust with the consumer, which creates a public interest to ensure activities are performed as advertised with appropriate minimum standards to minimize risk to consumers.
>
> It is CSBS policy that entities performing activities involving third party control of virtual currency should be subject to state licensure and supervision like an entity performing such activities with fiat currencies.[13]

Cryptocurrency presents a challenge to regulators because it can be utilized to perform activities involving third party control — activities that have long been performed with fiat currencies — yet unlike prior electronic financial tools, cryptocurrency can also be used for other unrelated purposes. It can be used by businesses to offer a financial service without having control of the customer's funds; it can be used by intermediaries to offer a non-financial service (such as a notary service); and it can be used by consumers directly and entirely without intermediaries.

Undoubtedly, some consumers will ask an intermediary to store and transmit their digital currency, and these intermediaries thereby assume a position of trust, which generates the basis for licensing and regulation. The key to developing such licensing and regulation, however, is to include those trusted intermediaries within a regulatory scheme while excluding others who do not assume that trust or do not offer financial services.

Intermediaries who do not assume a position of trust, non-financial uses, and individual access are digital currency innovations that should be encouraged. "Trustless" intermediaries can benefit both consumers and businesses through improved financial privacy, financial inclusion, and vibrant technology-based economies. These uses should not be burdened by compliance costs that lack concomitant consumer protection benefits.

---

[13] Conference of State Bank Supervisors, *State Regulatory Requirements for Vitrutal Currency Activities CSBS Model Regulatory Framework* 10, (Sep. 2015) *available at* https://www.csbs.org/regulatory/ep/Documents/CSBS-Model-Regulatory-Framework(September%2015%202015).pdf

Finally, some wonder whether cryptocurrencies like Bitcoin could have an impact on monetary policy. That seems unlikely, at least in the foreseeable future.

For Bitcoin to have any monetary effect it would have to become the widely used unit of account. This means that prices of goods, contracts, and loans would have to be denominated in Bitcoins rather than dollars. But as economist William Luther has shown, short of monetary catastrophe or government support, it's virtually impossible for a cryptocurrency to overcome the dollar's network effects, especially given the vast switching costs inherent in such a transition.[14]

Where Bitcoin may have monetary consequences is in countries like Argentina or Venezuela where capital controls have been a key part of the monetary policy. Many in those countries would like to escape the local currency to U.S. dollars, Swiss Francs, or gold, yet it is difficult to do so. Escaping to Bitcoin may be easier because of its censorship-resistance.

Conclusion

Bitcoin is only seven years old and it is still an experiment, but one that if successful will fundamentally change how we transact electronically. Like the Internet itself, Bitcoin has the potential to be a platform for the kind permissionless innovation that has driven so much of the growth of our economy. In fact, Bitcoin looks today very much like the Internet did in 1995. Some dismissed the Internet then as a curiosity, but many could see that such an open platform for innovation would allow for world-changing applications to be built on top of it. Few in 1995 could have foreseen Facebook or Skype or Netflix, but they could see that all the building blocks were there for some amazing innovations. Bitcoin is like that today. We cannot yet conceive what will be the killer applications of cryptocurrency, but it is plain that they will come.

Bitcoin faces some challenges, however, and chief among them is regulatory uncertainty. If we think back again to the early Internet, it was not until the government made it clear that it would pursue a light-touch regulatory approach that Internet innovation really took off. Bitcoin today is in need of a similar commitment from government.

If Coin Center could offer two guiding principles for you to use when considering policy related to Bitcoin they would be *clarity* and *innovation*. Clarity in terms of how existing regulations would apply to this new technology—rules of the road for innovators seeking to operate this space. And to always measure new policies against their impact on continued innovation. Like all emerging technologies, cryptocurrency also presents risks. The challenge governments face is to address those risks while doing no harm to the innovative potential of the technology.

---

[14] William J. Luther, "Cryptocurrencies, Network Effects, and Switching Costs," *Contemporary Economic Policy*, Oct. 16, 2015, *available at* http://onlinelibrary.wiley.com/doi/10.1111/coep.12151/abstract

If you need any further assistance as you consider cryptocurrencies, please do not hesitate to contact us at Coin Center. Our mission is to build a better understanding of these technologies and to promote a regulatory climate that preserves the freedom to innovate using blockchain technologies. We do this by producing and publishing policy research from respected academics and experts, by educating policymakers and the media about blockchain technology, and where appropriate advocacy for policies at the state and federal level consistent with our mission.

For your reference, included below is a list of some of Coin Center's plain-language backgrounders that you may wish to reference. More information is available on our website at CoinCenter.org. Also, attached to this letter is a copy of "Bitcoin: A Primer for Policymakers" that I hope will help you learn more about this technology.

Is Bitcoin Regulated? by Jerry Brito, Jan 13, 2015.
Coin Center Executive Director Jerry Brito debunks the common misconception about Bitcoin that it is not regulated. http://coincenter.org/2015/01/bitcoin-regulated/

How Anonymous is Bitcoin? by Adam Ludwin, Jan 20, 2015.
Adam Ludwin, Co-Founder of Chain.com, differentiates between anonymity and privacy in financial tools. http://coincenter.org/2015/01/anonymous-bitcoin/

How Are Payments with Bitcoin Different than Credit Cards? by Richard Gendal Brown, Jan 1, 2015.
Richard Gendal Brown compares paying with Bitcoin and paying with a credit card. http://coincenter.org/2015/01/payment-security/

What is Multi-Sig, and What Can It Do? by Ben Davenport, Jan 1, 2015.
Ben Davenport, co-founder at BitGo, simplifies the technical details of multi-signature transactions. http://coincenter.org/2015/01/multi-sig/

What is Bitcoin Mining, and Why is it Necessary? by Peter Van Valkenburgh, Dec 15, 2014.
Peter Van Valkenburgh, Coin Center's Director of Research, offers a plain English explanation of Bitcoin mining. http://coincenter.org/2014/12/bitcoin-mining/

What are Smart Contracts, and What Can We do with Them? by Houman Shadab, Dec 15, 2014.
New York Law School Professor and Coin Center Fellow Houman Shadab shares how block chains can make contracts "smart." http://coincenter.org/2014/12/smart-contracts/

How can Bitcoin be Used for Remittances? by Brock Cusick, Dec 2, 2014.
Attorney Brock Cusick describes the promise Bitcoin holds for sending money to one's home country. http://coincenter.org/2014/12/remittances/

Is Bitcoin's Price Volatility a Problem for the Technology? by Gil Luria, Dec 2, 2014.
Wedbush's Gil Luria shows why Bitcoin's notorious price volatility is not a surprise, nor a dilemma. http://coincenter.org/2014/12/volatility/

Are Consumer Bitcoin Balances Especially Vulnerable to Hacking? by Mike Belshe, Dec 1, 2014.
Mike Belshe, co-founder at BitGo, explains the risks facing consumers who hold Bitcoin. http://coincenter.org/2014/12/consumer-safety/

What are Colored Coins? by Brock Cusick, Nov 30, 2014.
Attorney Brock Cusick explains why a Bitcoin could be "colored" and potential applications of such coins. http://coincenter.org/2014/11/colored-coins/

Mr. BURGESS. The Chair thanks the gentleman.

Recognize Mr. Suarez for 5 minutes for your opening statement, please.

STATEMENT OF JUAN SUAREZ

Mr. SUAREZ. Chairman Burgess, Ranking Member, and members of the subcommittee, thank you very much for the opportunity to testify this morning on the role that virtual currency may play in disrupting today's financial services landscape.

My name is Juan Suarez, and I am counsel for Coinbase, the world's leading retail Bitcoin exchange platform. Coinbase was founded in early 2012 with the simple goal of becoming the easiest place to buy and sell Bitcoin. At the time of Coinbase's founding, one Bitcoin cost less than $10, virtual currency had not entered the mainstream, and little to no venture capital had been invested into the industry.

Today, 4 years later, one Bitcoin is valued at several hundred dollars, several leading online merchants accept Bitcoin as a means of payment from customers all over the world, and over $1 billion of venture capital has been invested into the space. We believe the rapid emergence of Bitcoin, together with other decentralized virtual currencies, is attributable to certain core characteristics that naturally orient the technology towards innovation and free and open use.

These characteristics include the following. First, decentralized virtual currencies are, by definition, distributed, meaning that perfect strangers may transact securely online without requiring the involvement of a trusted intermediary or a proprietary infrastructure. Second, virtual currencies are openly accessible via Internet-connected devices anywhere in the world. And, third, decentralized virtual currencies typically operate via an open source software protocol, and any software developer can build and independently own applications that facilitate new and innovative interactions among users.

These characteristics are strongly reminiscent of the early Internet, which began as an open network with modest underpinnings. They grew to revolutionize commerce and the way we communicate and which contributed untold billions or trillions of dollars to the United States economy.

Virtual currency, in our view, has the same promise. It has the fundamental capacity to expose entrenched financial services to unprecedented competition, to bring about new efficient and global consumer financial products, and, by virtue of very low marginal transaction costs, to unlock entire new industries never before realized.

Today we are still in the very early stages of virtual currency. The most widely adopted use of virtual currency thus far has been as an asset class for investing savings or for trading, but there are a great many additional applications of virtual currency with enormous promise.

And to just give you two examples, first, simply, as a means of payment for a good or service. Bitcoin rails have several advantages relative to customary online payment methods. Bitcoin is truly global, so a merchant can immediately accept payment from customers worldwide. Bitcoin is a push payment method. A merchant need not collect, and a customer need not provide sensitive payment credentials to settle a transaction.

This reduces proliferation of a customer's personal information and reduces the risk of catastrophic data breaches. And as a push payment, like handing over cash, there can be no fraudulent reversals, which cost online merchants billions of dollars in avoidable losses each year. This translates into savings.

Today, prominent payment processors that have integrated Bitcoin payment rails advertise processing fees less than one-third the cost of fees charged by those same processors to process card transactions. A second use case is remittance for peer-to-peer payments. Bitcoin and derivative technologies enable transactions that can be processed and settled at a cost of pennies, in some cases even less.

As of the time of this testimony, the fee associated with an average Bitcoin transaction is in the range of approximately 10 cents or below. That means a consumer can send, for example, $100 worth of Bitcoin anywhere in the world for just a few pennies. Today that same transaction would cost consumers around the globe on average more than $7 using conventional remittance services.

These and many other applications of virtual currencies are being actively pursued by thousands of developers all around the world, and we anticipate enormous innovation and growth in the virtual currency economy in coming years. And through the hard work of companies like Coinbase, together with core development teams, we can ensure that this innovation occurs in a safe and secure manner with cooperation among industry, consumer protection agencies, policymakers, and law enforcement.

Thanks very much, and I look forward to any questions you may have.

[The prepared statement of Mr. Suarez follows:]

22

TESTIMONY OF

Juan Suarez, Counsel

Coinbase, Inc.

BEFORE THE

United States House of Representatives Committee on Energy

and Commerce

Subcommittee on Commerce, Manufacturing, and Trade

"Disrupter Series: Digital Currency and Blockchain"

PRESENTED Rayburn House Office Building, Room 2123

March 16, 2016

11:00 AM

Chairman Burgess, Ranking Member Schakowsky, and Members of the Subcommittee: Thank you for the opportunity to testify this morning on the role that virtual currency may play in disrupting today's financial services landscape.

My name is Juan Suarez and I am Counsel for Coinbase, the world's leading retail bitcoin exchange platform. Coinbase was founded in early 2012 with the simple goal of becoming the easiest place to buy and sell bitcoin. At the time of Coinbase's founding, a bitcoin cost less than $10, virtual currency had not entered the mainstream, and little to no venture capital had been invested in the industry. Today, bitcoin has become the world's most preeminent virtual currency: one bitcoin is valued at several hundred dollars, the total value of all bitcoin in circulation exceeds $6 billion[1], and several leading online merchants accept bitcoin as a means of payment from customers all over the world.

We believe the rapid emergence of bitcoin, together with other decentralized virtual currencies, is attributable to several characteristics which, by design, naturally orient the technology towards innovation and free, open use. In particular, decentralized virtual currencies (*i*) are, by definition, decentralized, meaning that perfect strangers may transact reliably online without requiring the involvement of a trusted intermediary or its (proprietary) infrastructure and without necessarily disclosing personal information or payment credentials, (*ii*) typically operate via an-open sourced software protocol that anyone can study or to which anyone can submit proposed improvements, (*iii*) are accessible via internet-connected devices anywhere in the world, and (*iv*) allow any software developer to build (and independently own) applications that facilitate new and innovative interactions among users.

These characteristics are strongly reminiscent of the early Internet—itself a distributed network that facilitated unbounded global communication, innovation, and

---

[1] https://coinmarketcap.com

development of technologies never before imagined. Virtual currency has the fundamental capacity to expose closed and entrenched financial services providers to unprecedented competition, to bring about new, efficient, and global consumer financial products, and, through very low marginal transaction costs, to unlock entire new industries not previously realized. This enormous potential is the reason bitcoin and other emerging virtual currencies are often referred to as the "Internet of Money," and it is the reason why I am speaking to you today.

If it should please the subcommittee, I wish to share a few brief thoughts today about the promise of virtual currency, Coinbase's role in that ecosystem, our efforts to protect our customers and to guard against illicit activity, and finally, to share some of our concerns with emerging trends among policymakers.

Virtual Currency as Disruptor

To date, more than $1 billion has been invested by venture capital firms, large banks, and card networks, among others, into work on virtual currency or related "blockchain" technologies.[2] Since the invention of bitcoin in 2008, bitcoin has been debated, challenged, enhanced, and its initial distributed ledger innovation has led to the development of hundreds more virtual currencies. As of the time of this hearing, the combined market capitalization of the top 100 virtual currencies exceeds $8 billion.[3]

The most widely adopted use of virtual currency to date has been as an asset class for investing savings or for trading. In fact, over 80% of U.S. Coinbase transaction volume and roughly half of our U.S. users are engaged in investment activity—*i.e.*, they buy and hold bitcoin over the long term, or they trade on the Coinbase Exchange, our

---

[2] http://money.cnn.com/2015/11/02/technology/bitcoin-1-billion-invested/
[3] The top four virtual currencies—bitcoin, ethereum, ripple, and litecoin—account for over 95% of the total market capitalization of all virtual currencies combined. See https://coinmarketcap.com.

commercial bitcoin trading platform. Most virtual currency firms that generate revenue today operate similar trading platforms or retail conversion services.

There are, however, a great many additional uses of virtual currency beyond savings or investment activity. A worldwide race is underway to discover the "killer app"—a use of virtual currency so popular that it becomes an ordinary part of the everyday lives of tens of millions or even billions of people around the world. Although no single use case has achieved such popularity to date, several promising uses are emerging in parallel:

- *As a payment rail.* One of the most obvious applications of virtual currency is a means of payment for a good or service. Indeed, several large merchants have already enabled bitcoin payments on their platforms.[4] The bitcoin payment rails offer several advantages relative to common online payment methods: bitcoin is truly global, so a merchant can immediately accept payment from customers worldwide; bitcoin is a push payment method—a merchant need not collect (and a customer need not provide) sensitive payment credentials to process a payment; a bitcoin payment, once made, cannot be unilaterally clawed back by the payer, so common forms of costly, post-transaction payment reversal—*e.g.*, fraud chargebacks or insufficient funds—are not possible. Moreover, service providers can allow merchants to immediately convert bitcoin payments into local currency. Such providers, like Coinbase, can then batch local currency settlements to the merchant via low-priced, bank-to-bank transfers. The result is that the merchant receives payment in full, in dollars, at a much lower transaction cost, with little to no reversal risk, through a swift settlement window. These advantages translate directly into savings: payment processors that have

---

[4] More than 40,000 Coinbase users have enabled merchant tools to accept bitcoin payments. A select list of companies that use Coinbase to process bitcoin payments is available at https://www.coinbase.com/merchants.

integrated bitcoin as a payment rail advertise drastically lower processing fees relative to fees charged by the same processors for similar credit card processing services.[5]

- **As a remittance service**. Bitcoin's global nature and low marginal transaction costs open possibilities as a cross-border remittance tool. Even in the nascent stages, while conversion into local currency is required on both ends of the remittance transfer, several firms are exploring product offerings and use of peer networks to offer remittance and conversion services at competitive prices. In a world where bitcoin is widely accepted as a means of payment, then the process for sending money home becomes a triviality, like sending an e-mail. Further, the ease and relative thrift of global value transfer via virtual currency has led to the emergence of firms which seek to unlock cheap, global peer-to-peer credit markets, or peer contractor services for the provision of simple, often isolated tasks that can be performed cheaply and remotely.

- **As a micropayments tool**: Bitcoin and derivative technologies uniquely enable online transactions that can be processed and settled for pennies, in some cases even less.[6] These low transaction costs allow for economically viable micropayments that can unlock new incentive schemes (such as monetary incentives for small scale or one-off content creation, or peer tipping), new revenue models (such as *in-browser* micropayments that allows content hosts to seamlessly collect a small fee from visitors who wish to view a webpage rather

---

[5] See Stripe pricing at https://stripe.com/us/pricing (0.8% flat fee to process bitcoin payments vs. 2.9% + 30 cents for card payments); Braintree (beta) pricing at https://www.braintreepayments.com/features/coinbase (fee waived on first $1 million of transactions, then a 1% flat fee to process bitcoin payments vs. 2.9% + 30 cents for card payments).

[6] At the time of this writing, the fastest and cheapest typical bitcoin transaction will cost the sender a fee of about 0.00009 bitcoin, or approximately $0.03. See https://bitcoinfees.21.co/#fees (this fee ordinarily fluctuates with network conditions). Several companies are working on technologies that allow bitcoin transactions to occur more cheaply off-blockchain—*i.e.* which do not incur the typical bitcoin transaction fee and which can be processed for fractions of a penny.

than by monetizing via ad revenue), or even secure the way we communicate online (such as linking e-mails with tiny micropayments—an insignificant out-of-pocket cost to a typical user who sends several dozen (or hundreds) of e-mails daily, but which could render e-mail spamming operations economically unviable).

- **To settle property transfers**: More broadly, a hash value (a unique identifier) of any dataset can be uploaded to the bitcoin blockchain and can then be associated with bitcoin transfers through operation of the bitcoin network. The bitcoin blockchain can serve as an immutable, highly duplicated, and decentralized—*i.e.*, very secure—record of all transfers of such property. Several firms are investigating this use of bitcoin and related technologies to efficiently settle securities or other asset trades at low cost and high reliability. Others are investigating uses of smart contracts, or value transfer arrangements that can be programmed to self-execute via the blockchain based on certain preset criteria.

These and many other applications of virtual currencies are being actively pursued by *thousands* of developers around the world.[7] Put simply: we believe the invention of decentralized virtual currency is among the most historical breakthroughs in computer science, and its derivative technologies, commercial industries, and emergent mainstream products are likely to have as profound an impact on humanity as the Internet.[8]

We acknowledge a healthy debate has ensued over the design and operation of virtual currency protocols and related distributed ledger technology; some argue that certain characteristics of today's bitcoin protocol, such as low transaction fees and

---

[7] Descriptions of a few other promising bitcoin applications are available at: http://financialsingularity.com/top-apps/

[8] A useful introduction to the technology and its significance, authored by Marc Andreessen, was published in the New York Times dealbook on January 21, 2014, available at: http://dealbook.nytimes.com/2014/01/21/why-bitcoin-matters/.

28

transaction processing speed, may need to change in order to sustain continued transaction growth and/or continued decentralization of the network. In our view, healthy competition will emerge (and must emerge) among developer teams seeking to propose improvements to the bitcoin core protocol. Changes within bitcoin will be debated and voted upon by the processors (miners) comprising the bitcoin network, and through this process we believe an adaptive, competitive, and reliable decentralized virtual currency norm will emerge. We think bitcoin is likely to remain the world's leading virtual currency for some time—and to date, it is the only virtual currency we have supported on our platform—but Coinbase's ultimate goal is to afford our users convenient access to the most popular virtual currency(s), and we may well support additional virtual currencies in response to consumer demand.

Finally, several companies have invested resources into distributed ledger technology which does not necessarily involve decentralized virtual currency. Many proposals seem to involve centralized control and coordination by one party, proprietary interests over the network, and limited points of access for third-party development. Although these technologies would appear to forfeit some of the core, innovation-friendly characteristics of decentralized virtual currency—indeed, some leading investors have expressed reasoned skepticism that "permissioned ledgers" will have a transformative impact[9]—Coinbase looks forward to learning whether other competent firms' work on permissioned ledgers will lead to improved distributed database technology or settlement tools that can reduce the cost of incumbent financial services.

---

[9] Marc Andreessen, co-founder, Andreessen Horowitz, December 17, 2015, twitter ("Big companies desperately hoping for blockchain without Bitcoin is exactly like 1994: Can't we please have online without Internet??"); Glenn Hutchins, co-founder, Silver Lake Partners, January 16, 2015 ("The private ledger is equivalent to the *intranet*. Remember when we first had intranet? It was kind of good because you could collaborate with people you work with but it didn't transform things until everybody was connected in the seamless world wide web."); reported at: http://www.newsbtc.com/2016/01/17/glenn-hutchins-you-cant-have-the-blockchain-without-bitcoin/.

Coinbase's Role in the Virtual Currency Ecosystem

Today, Coinbase operates the world's largest retail conversion service with over three million users around the world. Our retail bitcoin conversion services are available to customers in thirty-two countries where, with the assistance of banking or other payment processor partners, Coinbase can accept local currency payments via local bank transfers or debit cards. To date, our customers have bought or sold more than $3.5 billion-worth of bitcoin through our platform and we safe keep more customer bitcoin than likely any other commercial enterprise in the world. Our company is headquartered in San Francisco, we have over 100 employees, and we have raised over $100 million from leading venture capital firms, major banks, and the New York Stock Exchange.[10]

We generate revenue solely through transaction fees we charge customers to purchase or sell bitcoin on the Coinbase platform—for retail users, typically a flat, 1% fee. We do not attempt to profit by adding margins to market exchange rates, nor do we charge users to store bitcoin on Coinbase or transact in bitcoin.

Coinbase's long-term success depends upon, first, the increasing adoption of virtual currency and, second, maintaining the continued trust of our customers, bank partners, and regulators. For Coinbase, these twin criteria are linked: our contribution towards establishing a scalable ecosystem is to provide a reliable, trustworthy, safe, and transparent platform which enables customers around the world to efficiently acquire or liquidiate virtual currency. We invest considerable resources towards this goal: we invest in customer support and consumer best-practices comparable to norms in the regulated consumer financial services space; we constantly enhance and scrutinize the security of customer and corporate assets and data; we work extremely closely with our banks and

---

[10] https://blog.coinbase.com/2015/01/20/coinbase-raises-75m-from-dfj-growth-usaa-nyse/.

other payment processors in order to enable convenient local payments (to acquire bitcoin) in a user's local currency; we employ professional investigations staff and robust compliance tools to monitor our platform for suspicious activity and to coordinate with law enforcement; we have met with many agencies of state and federal government to train agents and policymakers in the operation of Coinbase's platform and virtual currency generally; and in many U.S. jurisdictions, certain of Coinbase products constitute regulated financial services (more below). I highlight two areas of particular operational importance to Coinbase which are most relevant to many other virtual currency trading platforms and policymakers: consumer protection and anti-money laundering.

Consumer Protection

We are keenly aware that virtual currency, like any early-stage technology, is prone towards abusive practices. Some consumer abuse results from unscrupulous merchants who accept bitcoin as a means of a payment from customers who cannot reverse a fraudulent transaction; other abuse stems from virtual currency service providers themselves who fail to properly secure customer assets from theft or fraud.[11]

Avoiding both types of abuse on our platform is paramount to customer trust. In brief: Coinbase vets merchants whose transactions we process. We reject merchants who appear at risk of deceptive or abusive practices or who may be in violation of Coinbase's prohibited businesses policies, we monitor merchants' continued use of the platform, and in certain circumstances, we may become involved in remediation of merchant disputes if appropriate. In addition, Coinbase does not expose its customers' payment credentials to Coinbase merchants (unless expressly requested by the

---

[11] The FTC, for example, has warned of the unregulated nature of most bitcoin operations and has stated that it has received reports of unfair practices among certain abusive merchants who accept bitcoin as payment. See blog posts dated June 22, 2015, available at https://www.consumer.ftc.gov/blog/paying-bitcoins, and September 23, 2014, available at https://www.consumer.ftc.gov/blog/staying-current-bitcoin-and-other-cryptocurrencies.

customer), so even if a merchant is independently subject to a data breach, customer payment data is unaffected.

Separately, Coinbase implements and audits security procedures pertaining to bitcoin storage, application security, infrastructure and network security, user account security (we require strong, two-factor authentication on all new logins and new device verification, among other safeguards), employee access and physical security, and customer data. These protocols are time consuming and expensive, and in fact, there is no formally established best practice for virtual currency security. We believe that best practices will emerge—and emerge quickly—as leaders in the industry begin to adopt uniform and consistently audited security practices. I will highlight one aspect of our security program which is common among many leading virtual currency platforms: bitcoin cold storage. Approximately 99% of customer bitcoin is stored offline and cannot be transferred without restoring it, in complete and readable form, to an Internet-accessed device. A quorum of multiple individuals' active authorization is required to restore and decrypt the bitcoin private keys held in cold storage and thus to unlock the associated bitcoin for transfer off platform. This procedure is a critical line of defense against Mt. Gox-style hacks and can avoid significant consumer loss. In addition, Coinbase is one of the few companies in the world to have private insurance against loss or theft of the small percentage of customer bitcoin is connected to the Internet.

Preventing Money Laundering

Coinbase and all other decentralized virtual currency exchangers are required to register as a Money Services Business ("MSBs"). As such, Coinbase maintains a Bank Secrecy Act ("BSA") Anti-Money Laundering ("AML") / Know-Your-Customer ("KYC") program. We report primarily to the Financial Crimes Enforcement Network ("FinCEN") within the U.S. Department of the Treasury, and like other MSBs, we are subject to federal auditing of our BSA program.

It is critical to Coinbase that we protect our platform from illicit actors who may attempt to cash out proceeds of dark web, black market commerce. To that end, Coinbase's Chief Compliance Officer maintains a customer information and onboarding program that enables Coinbase to identify its customers and monitor for suspicious activity. We train all staff in AML procedures, we subject our compliance program to regular internal testing and independent, annual review by third-party auditors, and we work closely with law enforcement agents. Coinbase is particularly proud to have built and designed unique in-house tools that enable our investigations team to more effectively and programmatically monitor customer behavior, including our customers' interaction with the bitcoin blockchain.

Emerging Regulation

At the federal level, Coinbase registers with and reports to FinCEN. At the state level, Coinbase has sought licensure of certain of its products under existing state money transmission regimes[12]. We think a measured approach to virtual currency regulation should begin with an appreciation for the small size of the virtual currency economy relative to existing financial services. To take one perspective, the Visa network alone processed 71 billion transactions in 2015 for a total payment and cash volume of $7.4 trillion[13]—this averages to 194 million daily transactions whose combined value exceeds $20 billion. And that's just one card network. PayPal, as another example, reported approximately 4.9 billion transactions worth $282 billion in 2015, for a

---

[12] Coinbase is currently licensed to engage in money transmission in 32 U.S. jurisdictions. A majority of these jurisdictions license Coinbase to operate a PayPal-style U.S. Dollar, stored value facility. Coinbase customers use this U.S. Dollar facility to settle trades on the Coinbase Exchange. A minority of these jurisdictions—fewer than ten—have indicated that operation of certain other products, including hosted bitcoin wallets and Coinbase's bitcoin conversion service, *also* fall within the scope of licensed activity. For those states, a much larger scope of services ostensibly fall within the scope of prudential oversight. New York is the unequivocal leader in this category. Coinbase's application to engage in virtual currency business activity in the state of New York (the "BitLicense") is currently pending.

[13] See Visa's 2015 annual report, available at:
http://s1.q4cdn.com/050606653/files/doc_financials/annual/VISA-2015-Annual-Report.pdf

daily average transaction count exceeding 13 million and volume exceeding $770 million.[14] By contrast, the entire bitcoin network processes on the order of 200,000 to 275,000 transactions per day, with an estimated value in the range of $200 million[15]. In other words, all daily transactions processed via the bitcoin network—far and away the largest virtual currency network in the world—amount to roughly 1% of Visa's daily transaction count and volume, and less than one third the amount of PayPal.

In short: the virtual currency economy is clearly in its infancy.

Although we acknowledge that a money laundering risk exists at the points of virtual currency and fiat currency exchange, the magnitude of worldwide consumer risk exposure to virtual currency, relative to existing financial services, is low. To the extent any prudential oversight is deemed appropriate at this early stage, Coinbase feels that operators in this space who are entrusted to sell, store, and transfer virtual currency on behalf of customers can be regulated adequately under existing money transmission regimes—*i.e.*, regimes that have been adopted to regulate companies with innovative stored value and other money transfer products, like PayPal. Although wholesale adoption of money transmission laws or other existing regulatory structures is not possible in every case—some states' laws are vary narrowly drafted—we believe that methodical adjustments to state money transmission rules or laws can effectively and efficiently leverage existing protections to promote fair, sound, and safe business practices among standard hosted wallet and retail conversion services.[16] Of course, the offering of more complex products may be appropriate for consideration for licensure under different state or federal charters.

---

[14] See PayPal's Form 10-K for fiscal year ending December 31, 2015, available at https://investor.paypal-corp.com/.
[15] https://blockchain.info/charts/n-transactions and https://blockchain.info/charts/estimated-transaction-volume-usd.
[16] For a further explanation, see Coinbase's February 26, 2015 letter to the Conference of State Bank Supervisors, available at https://www.csbs.org/regulatory/ep/pages/framework.aspx.

We have identified two particular areas where regulatory overreach, both at the state level, may seriously jeopardize the success of virtual currency businesses in the United States. First, any regulatory construct that contemplates a dual licensing process is potentially wasteful, unnecessary, and overly burdensome. For example, a virtual currency business who also holds customers' dollars may be required to obtain, in some states, both a "traditional" license to engage in money transmission activity *and* a "virtual currency" license, even notwithstanding the fact that the respective purpose of each regime is to achieve essentially the same outcome, via similar diligence processes, administered by the same regulator. Second, inefficiency and avoidable cost stems from the unnecessary duplication of reporting and KYC obligations arising under federal law. In particular, we believe AML regulation and reporting is best coordinated by FinCEN. Although it is certainly the prerogative of state regulators to require licensees to comply with applicable federal law and to conduct audits accordingly, we believe the imposition of state-specific, bespoke anti-money laundering obligations constitutes a bold and costly departure from the prevailing norm, and does not necessarily offer enhanced law enforcement tools relative to a centralized reporting structure managed by the Treasury.

Conclusion

Thank you for the opportunity to testify today. Coinbase looks forward to continued work with policymakers as the virtual currency industry becomes a larger and exciting part of our United States and world economy. I look forward to answering any questions you may have.

Mr. BURGESS. The Chair thanks the gentleman.

Mr. Cuomo, recognized for 5 minutes for your opening statement, please.

STATEMENT OF JERRY CUOMO

Mr. CUOMO. Good morning, Chairman Upton, Ranking Member Pallone, Chairman Burgess, Ranking Member Schakowsky, and members of the subcommittee. My name is Jerry Cuomo, and I am the Vice President for Blockchain Technologies at IBM. And thank you very much for the opportunity to testify this morning.

We at IBM believe that blockchain is a revolutionary technology. With blockchain we can reimagine many of the world's most fundamental business interactions, and at the same time open the door to new styles of digital interactions that we have yet to even imagine. You are wise to include blockchain in your study of disruptive technologies, because blockchain has the potential to vastly reduce the cost and complexity of getting things done across industries, Government agencies, and social institutions.

I also want to tell you what blockchain is not. It is not Bitcoin, the crypto-currency. While blockchain is the core technology that enables Bitcoin to operate, it can be used for entirely different purposes. Whereas Bitcoin operates as an anonymous network, blockchain can be used as a trusted network to handle interactions with known parties.

It is our strong feeling that the benefits of blockchain are realized in its broadest use, across the broadest set of industries, from supply chain to trade settlement, from tax to land deeds, birth certificates and social security. This morning my testimony makes four points, which I will summarize now.

The first point is about how blockchain changes the game. At the center of a blockchain is the notion of a shared ledger. Think of this as one of those little black accounting books. However, this book has seemingly magical properties. You see, members of a blockchain network each have an exact copy of the ledger. New entries in the ledger are instantaneously propagated throughout the network. Therefore, all participants in an interaction have an up-to-date ledger that reflects the most recent transactions, and the transactions, once entered, cannot be changed.

Now, let me tell you why and how blockchain actually changes the game. Transactions can now be settled instantaneously versus in days. Cost is reduced due to elimination of middlemen. And because of how these transactions are stored on the ledger, the chances of tampering and collusion are greatly reduced.

My next point is blockchain technologies must be made enterprise-ready. The core blockchain technology must focus on security and privacy concerns that arise within enterprise use cases. In addition, computer systems and networks must be architected so they scale up and can handle immense volumes of transactions. Simply put, we in IBM are openly working with a group of industry collaborators to build a new blockchain from the ground up, with privacy, confidentiality, scaleability, and auditability, front and center. This is what enterprise-ready means, which leads me to my third point.

Blockchain must be open. For blockchain to fulfill its potential, it must be based on nonproprietary technology. And doing so will encourage broad adoption and ensure compatibility and interoperability of systems. Specifically, this enterprise-ready blockchain must be built using open source software with a combination of liberal licensing terms and strict governance. Only with openness will blockchain be widely adopted and enable innovation.

We are participating with over 30 industry players in the Hyperledger Project led by the Linux Foundation to create an open, enterprise-ready blockchain.

And my last point is blockchain will greatly benefit from Government participation. Blockchain holds the promise of enabling more effective interactions between Government and business. For example, working as an invited member of an enterprise blockchain, Government agencies could be able to better collaborate in financial and commercial systems, and spot potential problems before they become critical, regarding everything from tax to land use.

So it is critical that U.S. companies and Government agencies lead the world in demonstrating the potential of blockchain.

Now, I should add that blockchain isn't the answer to everything. There will be situations where it will improve efficiencies, but there will be others where it is simply not a good fit. Furthermore, we should not underestimate the technical and organizational challenges of building and adopting blockchain systems.

Blockchain is a classic emergent technology, but it is so strikingly different from what people are used to that many leaders are adopting a wait-and-see attitude. Now, we applaud judicious caution, but now is the time to quickly assess the potential of blockchain and begin experimenting. Therefore, we urge Congress and the Obama administration to study and discover the best uses of blockchain for the U.S. Government.

We also want to pay attention to regulatory approaches to maximize its potential while protecting the interest of citizens. Blockchain may have begun its existence as the underpinning of the crypto-currency, but now it stands in the open, a powerful tool ready to serve business and society.

And thank you again for your invitation and I would be glad to answer any questions you have.

[The prepared statement of Mr. Cuomo follows:]

Gennaro (Jerry) Cuomo

IBM Fellow

Vice President, Blockchain Technologies

House Energy and Commerce

Subcommittee on Commerce, Manufacturing & Trade

How to Capitalize on Blockchain

March 16, 2016

Good Morning Chairman Upton, Ranking Member Pallone, Chairman Burgess, Ranking Member

Schakowsky, and members of the subcommittee. My name is Jerry Cuomo and I am IBM's Vice President

for Blockchain Technologies. Thank you very much for the opportunity to testify this morning.

Technology and business leaders at IBM believe that blockchain is a revolutionary technology. It's a

foundation for building a new generation of applications that establish trust and transparency while

streamlining a wide variety of transactional processes. You are wise to include blockchain in your study

of "disruptive" technologies because blockchain has the potential to vastly reduce the cost and

complexity of getting things done—across industries, government agencies and social institutions.

I also want to tell you what blockchain is not, It's not Bitcoin, the cryptocurrency. While blockchain is the

core technology that enables Bitcoin to operate, it can be used for entirely different purposes. Whereas

Bitcoin is an anonymous network, blockchain can be used to set up trusted networks to handle

interactions between known parties.

In this paper I'll explain what blockchain is, how it works, how it can best be built and used—for the

benefit of business, the economy and society.

Key points:

Blockchain creates trustworthy and efficient interactions. It's a distributed ledger shared via a peer-to-peer network that maintains an ever-expanding list of data records. Each participant has an exact copy of the ledger's data, and additions to the chain are propagated throughout the network. Therefore, all participants in an interaction have an up-to-date ledger that reflects the most recent transactions or changes. (The "block" is the record and the "chain" is the collection of blocks that populate the ledger.) In this way, Blockchain reduces the need for establishing trust using traditional methods.

Blockchain technologies must be enhanced to meet the needs of businesses. The core technology must be adapted to further address security and privacy concerns—creating an enterprise-ready blockchain. In addition, computer systems and networks must be architected so they can scale up to handle an immense volume of transactions and industries and governments begin using the technology to handle their core organizational processes—and complete their tasks in seconds rather than minutes.

Blockchains must be open and interoperable. For blockchain to fulfill its full potential, it must be based on non-proprietary technology standards to assure the compatibility and interoperability of systems. Furthermore, the various blockchain versions should be built using open source software, with a combination of liberal licensing terms and strict governance, rather than proprietary software--which could be used to suppress competition. Only with openness will blockchain be widely adopted and will innovation flourish.

Blockchain will greatly benefit from government participation. It's critical from a national competiveness point of view for US companies and government agencies to lead the world in understanding the potential of blockchain and putting it to use. Because of the transparency made possible by blockchain, government agencies will be able to understand better what's going on within financial and commercial systems—and spot potential problems before they become critical. Blockchain will also enable more efficient interactions between government and businesses—regarding everything from taxes to land use.

Part 1: How Blockchain Can Be Used

Over the past two decades, the Internet, cloud computing and related technologies have revolutionized many aspects of business and society. These advances have made individuals and organizations more productive, and they have enriched many people's lives.

Yet the basic mechanics of how people and organizations forge agreements with one another and execute them have not been updated for the 21st century. In fact, with each passing generation we've added more middlemen, more processes, more bureaucratic checks and balances, and more layers of complexity to our formal interactions—especially financial transactions. We're pushing old procedures through new pipes.

This apparatus—the red tape of modern society—extracts a "tax" of many billions of dollars per year on the global economy and businesses.

What can be done? Businesses, governments and other institutions can use blockchains to build and govern business networks..

Blockchain-based systems could help radically improve whole industries, beginning with banking and insurance. But its impact could be much broader. It could make a difference whenever valuable assets are transferred from one party to another and whenever you need to know for certain that a piece of digital information — anything from electronic artwork to the terms of a business agreement — is unique and unchangeable by any party without the agreement of all parties.

I want to add a note of caution, however. Blockchain isn't the answer to every process- or transaction-related problem. There will be situations where it will improve efficiencies and provide other benefits, but there will be others where it's not a good fit. Furthermore, don't underestimate the technical and organizational challenges of building and adopting blockchain-based systems.

Here's where blockchain fits well—managing a business agreement between two or more companies. They can record the terms of that agreement on a blockchain, knowing it will execute and be enforced autonomously (e.g., "if you pay me in under 15 days, then I will give you a discount."). Nobody is in private control of the ledger and nobody can secretly change the terms of the agreement. It's like every guest at a B&B writing in the guest book with an indelible Sharpie. So, with blockchain, facts and agreements are recorded certifiably and indelibly, increasing trust, reducing risk, and thus reducing friction in business.

There's a broad range of potential business solutions. On one hand, enterprises will be able to re-imagine well known business processes and areas like supply chain, securities trading and logistics. At the same time, blockchain is poised to enable enterprises and whole industries to invent new digital business processes that include connected devices (Internet of Things) like cars, smartphones, appliances, solar energy panels, and drones. This capability could be critical, for instance, in enabling the insurance industry to design liability insurance policies to cover autonomous vehicles.

IBM is already begun deploying a blockchain-based system internally—for managing our commercial financing business.

The financial services industry is in the forefront of blockchain adoption. Almost every transaction in financial services involves multiple parties and many steps, largely because of the checks and balances that are required to assure that what has been promised has been done. Consider how the technology might be used in a critical financial services process, the settlement in securities trading. People in the industry are talking about a concept they call T+0, which means same day settlement. The hope is that they'll be able to use blockchain to strip out the inefficiencies and handoffs that are required to settle a trade so that settlement occurs on the same day as opposed to 2 or 3 days later as it is today, depending on the market.

Now, imagine supply chains where blockchain is put to work. An aircraft manufacturer, for example, might create a blockchain-based system for holistically managing all of its relationships with suppliers of parts and components. All of the suppliers will share the exact same information about a new aircraft model—every step in the process of planning, designing, assembling, delivering and maintaining it. At the same time, the manufacturer will use other blockchain-based systems for managing the financial relationships and transactions connected to each step. Thanks to blockchain, trust and accountability are built into supply chains. So are compliance with government regulations and internal rules and processes.

Blockchain fundamentally changes the game across three dimensions: time, cost, and risk. It reduces the time required to settle a multi-party contract from days to seconds, potentially. It reduces costs by stripping out intermediary organizations and processes. And, by enabling permissioned networks to share a transparent and non-changeable ledger, you reduce the risk of tampering, fraud and collusion.

Part 2: How Blockchain Works

Blockchain is both a software technology and a mechanism for groups working together.

At the heart of the blockchain network is a shared ledger, which describes assets, identifies their owners, lays out the steps in a process and records when each step is completed. Only at that point is the exchange of things of value consummated. The ledger has three important properties: replication, which synchronizes all of the copies of the ledger in the network; consensus, which assures that all ledgers are exact copies; and permissions, which ensure that members of a network can only see items in ledger that involve them.

When an entry is agreed to and committed to the blockchain's shared ledger, it cannot be changed. This is a critical feature, which differentiates blockchain's ledger from most database technologies--where entries can be updated and deleted. This makes blockchain resistant to tampering and provides clear audit trails for parties in transactions and government investigators to follow.

Another critical element of blockchain technology is the "smart contract." These are terms of agreement that are captured in software and stored and executed within the blockchain. The smart contracts automatically fulfill the obligations that members have agreed to. A blockchain is an ideal place to store and run such contracts because of its immutability and cryptographic security.

In our view, however, most blockchain implementations, and the tools surrounding them, aren't yet ready for many serious business uses. The concept and architecture are taking form, but some key capabilities and standards are missing or only now emerging. For instance, many enterprise applications require more extensive security capabilities than most of today's blockchain implementations offer. Within healthcare, more extensive privacy protections are needed.

So IBM and others in the industry are augmenting the core blockchain technologies with additional features. One goal is to ensure that institutions and individuals (whether participants or not) can only access information they're supposed to see. A key element is "entitled access," which is achieved by using modern cryptography so access to private data requires presentation of encryption keys/certificates held by authorized participants.

We're also taking steps to ensure that participants cannot commit fraud or collude in ways that jeopardize the integrity of the blockchain. Fraud and collusion resistance is achieved by ensuring that every transaction is validated by all the members of the blockchain networks, which might include regulatory and clearinghouse institutions.

Lastly, we're enabling regulators , with permission, to check for regulatory compliance, and for law enforcement with proper judicial authority, to access details of transactions in the course of criminal investigations.

These additional features will be essential in healthcare scenarios, where the privacy of individuals is both a legal and moral imperative. Blockchain can prevent against accidental or malicious privacy breaches by requiring both encryption and multiple signatures to approve access to sensitive information. There might be a mechanism, for instance, that for a patient record to be seen, a doctor, a nurse and the patient must approve within the blockchain.

Part 3: Why it's Critical for Blockchains to be Open and Interoperable

It's essential for blockchain technology to be developed following the open source model so a critical mass of organizations will coalesce around it—and reap its full benefits. Because of open source rules, participants can trust that the technology will fulfill their needs and conform with industry standards— assuring interoperability between blockchain applications. Also, by sharing the foundational layer, the participants can focus their individual efforts on industry-specific applications, platforms, and hardware systems to support transactions.

An open source blockchain with liberal licensing terms and strict governance will enable the broadest adoption of blockchain by regulated industries. The liberal licensing terms will accelerate innovation, and the strict governance will hasten adoption and regulatory acceptance.

Given the nature of a blockchain network, industry users and regulators of blockchain are going to want visibility right down to the source code to verify its source, accuracy and security.

We believe that the best path forward for blockchain is for the tech industry, government, and the business community to consolidate their efforts around a single open source blockchain foundation that's developed and governed in an environment of transparency and cooperation. We also believe that organizations will be best served if they use industry-specific or function-specific extensions of that technology, which are created and governed following the same principles. An example of this might be a banking framework that deals with loans, lenders and borrowers.

There are several open source blockchain projects, but only the project managed and sanctioned by the Linux Foundation, called Linux Hyperledger, offers industry friendly terms and multi-company governance. That's why we're participating in the Linux Hyperledger project and urging others to do so as well.

The Linux Foundation announced the project last December. Founding members of the initiative represent a diverse group of stakeholders, including ABN AMRO, Accenture, ANZ Bank, BNY Mellon, Cisco, The Depository Trust & Clearing Corporation (DTCC), Deutsche Börse Group, Digital Asset Holdings, Fujitsu Limited, IBM, Intel, J.P. Morgan, R3, Red Hat, SWIFT, VMware and Wells Fargo. Already, several companies, including IBM, have contributed high-quality software code, technology, and intellectual property rights. The transparency, collaboration and shared governance of this project makes it attractive to participants—whether they're technology companies or enterprises who want to deploy the technology. The reaction to the announcement was overwhelming. More than 2300 organizations or individuals have asked to participate, the highest such tally in the Linux Foundation's history.

Part 4: Government's Stake in Blockchain

Blockchain is a true technology phenomenon. Less than a year ago, it was little known outside a small group of technologists. Now, it's making headlines everywhere and businesses and governments are scrambling to come to terms with it.

The good news for government leaders is that Blockchain has the potential to transform governmental processes as fundamentally as is does those of the businesses—providing superior levels of transparency, accuracy and efficiency. It could help governments do everything from collect taxes and deliver social services benefits, to manage land registries and assure the integrity of government records.

Take the US Social Security system, for instance. It involves the federal government, millions of employers, their payroll service providers, and more than 200 million beneficiaries and working individuals who are paying into the system. This is a model scenario for blockchain. There are many parties, many rules, many steps in the process of administering the system, and a critical need for very high levels of privacy protection and security from breaches.

Other potential uses of the technology are quite intriguing. What if the US government began issuing regulations and monitoring compliance via blockchain technology? And what if the government implemented the taxation system with blockchain. Individuals and businesses might never have to file an income tax return. Instead, a blockchain network noting their tax obligations and recording their financial transactions would continuously invoke the tax code, assess taxes and transfer money. No need to file a tax return.

The possibilities are endless, yet most governments around the world have not yet begun to come to terms with blockchain.

In my view, there's a clear role for government—cribbed liberally from a position paper issued recently by the UK government. It should:

Use blockchain technology. Government should act as an early adopter and start deploying the technology for projects like voting, recording land registries, managing immigration, and the like

Invest in research. Just as the National Institute of Standards and Technology works with industry to develop and apply technology, measurements, and standards, the government should investigate to make sure blockchain technology is robust, secure and scalable, while understanding the ethical and social implications of potential uses and the costs and benefits of adoption.

Create a regulation framework. The government needs to make sure that blockchains are being used in accordance with US laws while avoiding the stifling of innovation through excessive or rigid regulations.

Set standards to ensure security and privacy. The government needs to work with academia and industry to ensure that standards are set for the integrity, security and privacy of distributed ledgers and their contents. These standards need to be reflected in both regulatory and software code.

Conclusion

Blockchain is a classic emergent technology. It appears to have a broad set of uses and benefits, but it's so strikingly different from what people are used to that many business and government leaders alike are adopting a wait-and-see attitude. We applaud judicious caution, but, at the same time, we believe that organizations and institutions that don't quickly assess the potential of blockchain and begin experimenting with it risk falling behind as the world undergoes what we see as a tectonic shift.

Therefore, we urge Congress and the Obama administration to study and discover the best uses of blockchain for the US government and the best regulatory approaches to maximizing its potential while protecting the interests of citizens. Blockchain may have begun its existence in the shadows of the crypto currency realm, but it now stands in the open—a powerful tool ready to serve business and society.

Mr. BURGESS. The Chair thanks the gentleman.

Mr. Snow, you are recognized for 5 minutes, please.

STATEMENT OF PAUL SNOW

Mr. SNOW. Thank you, Chairman Burgess and members of the subcommittee for the opportunity to testify before you today. I am Paul Snow, the Chief Architect of Factom, a protocol to provide blockchain solutions to a wide range of problems above and beyond simple currency transactions.

Let me do something strange here. I am a developer, and so I am going to talk to you about what a blockchain really is and——

Mr. BURGESS. Mr. Snow, I hate to interrupt. Just be sure your microphone is on. I think——

Mr. SNOW. You know, I might be on now. Do I need to reset? OK.

Well, I am going to do something strange here, and I am going to try to help you guys be developers like I am. I am going to actually explain to you what a blockchain is. OK?

First and foremost, if you don't understand hashing functions, you will never understand blockchains. Now that is scary, so let me tell you what a hashing function is. Any piece of data at all—a picture, a video, even your signature, your address—any piece of data at all can be mathematically constructed to create a very small fingerprint, and that fingerprint is unique for that piece of data.

If I make one little change to that data, I will get a completely different fingerprint, and no fingerprint of any two data sets, no hash of two different data sets, has ever matched. This is called no collisions. There is no collisions. So fingerprint, certain data. Change it, break the fingerprint.

Now, we talk about blockchains, so what is a block? Well, block is a lot of data. It is a lot of transactions, but it could also be records, it could be records for a mortgage, it could be the process by which you validate a land title in a land titling system. It is just a bunch of data.

Now, we make blocks. We take a bunch of this data, and we put it together. That is a block. And guess what we do to it? We hash it. Now, what have we done when we hashed it? We have created a block of data you never get to change again, because if you change it, you will break the hash.

Now, what do we do with a hash? Well, we will put it in the next block, and then we will collect some more data. Now, that is the chain in blockchain. It is a chain of blocks completely tied down and secured against any modification in the future by the hash that is in the next block in the chain. And as I progress and collect more data, nobody gets to change the past, and that is really the magic of blockchain.

So what can I do with blockchains? I can do a lot of stuff. Can I secure a lot of data? Well, yes, because there is this other trick we can do with hashes, and that is we can have a tournament. How many of you have been to a tournament before? Have you ever seen a tournament bracket? You can follow your team all the way from the beginning, competing against thousands of other teams, all the way to its winner slot. Your team always wins, right? All the way to the winning slot, and all I have to consider is that team and the games it plays in. I don't have to look at all of those other participants.

Ms. SCHAKOWSKY. Can Cub fans do that, too?

Mr. SNOW. What is that?

Ms. SCHAKOWSKY. Can Cub fans——

Mr. SNOW. Cub fans, yes, they can. Sometimes the chain is a little shorter.

So the idea is I can take a ton of data, and I can create one— I can combine—instead of games that are hashes, I can end up with one hash at the end that secures a ton of data, and there is a small path to any piece of data that proves that data hasn't changed. I don't have to look at everything.

Factom is built on that. That is the protocol that I am building, and I build a collection of these Merkle Trees, these tournament brackets, for data that is collected, and I place that hash in a public witness. And the public witness in this case is Bitcoin blockchain, because it has the most secure data structure on the planet right now.

But we can also go put it in IBM's Hyperledger or in Ethereum or many other blockchains, and we create a basis by which you can write an application that runs in the context of a private chain within all the security that we need for some applications. And it can access vast sums of data, like weather data, like transactions on exchanges, huge sets of data, and prove that that data is historically correct and accurate. And that is basically the power of the blockchain is to create histories that you can trust that can be validated and verified and can be used across many different systems.

And I will be happy to answer any questions anybody has. And if you want to apply as a programmer, I can certainly talk to you about that, too. Thank you very much.

[The prepared statement of Mr. Snow follows:]

Paul Snow
Chief Architect, Co-Founder
Factom Inc.
Disrupter Series: Digital Currency and Blockchain Technology
before
The Committee on Energy and Commerce Subcommittee on Commerce, Manufacturing
and Trade
U.S. House of Representatives
March 16, 2016

Thank you Chairman Burgess and members of the Subcommittee for the opportunity to testify before you

today. I am Paul Snow, the chief Architect of Factom, a protocol focused on lowering the costs and barriers

to creating new Blockchain based solutions, as well as applying Blockchain based solutions to existing

systems.

Blockchain based technology has been cited as disruptive by the Brookings Institution[1], Deloitte[2], Goldman

Sachs[3], and many others. The open source protocol Bitcoin Blockchain was launched into the computer

ecosystem in 2009. By 2012 the disruptive nature of this protocol was becoming evident. Bitcoin the

currency was just the beginning of a more general revolution in how we approach data security, settlement,

business process audits, and more.

Through Cryptographic checks and distributed ledgers, we can advance financial reform, increase

efficiency, reduce costs, increase privacy, and oddly enough, reduce crime and money laundering. I was

quite surprised by the warm reception many three letter agencies afforded crypto currency and Blockchains.

---

[1] Beyond bitcoin: The future of blockchain and disruptive financial technologies
http://www.brookings.edu/events/2016/01/14-beyond-bitcoin-blockchain-disruptive-financial-technologies

[2] Banking reimagined How disruptive forces will radically transform the industry in the decade ahead
http://www2.deloitte.com/content/dam/Deloitte/us/Documents/financial-services/us-fsi-banking-industry-outlook-2016.pdf

[3] Emerging Theme Radar: What if I Told You... http://www.goldmansachs.com/our-thinking/pages/macroeconomic-insights-folder/what-if-i-told-you/report.pdf

at the Department of Justice's Digital Currency Conference held at the Federal Reserve in San Francisco last year.

Allow me to cover a few points about the technology behind Blockchains that might not be obvious. First of all, Blockchains utilize Hash functions to link together blocks of information. A Hash is a way of taking any digital artifact, a document, picture, video, transaction, etc. and producing a short digital fingerprint. A block is a collection of transactions, and can include these fingerprints and other digital data. When a block is added to a Blockchain, the hash of the previous block is also included in the new block. That's the "Chain" part of Blockchains. Validating a Blockchain includes checking the hashes or the fingerprints, and making sure they match. Any error or change in data would "break" the chain; the hash of the changed block would no longer match the hash in the next block in the chain.

Since we can hash anything digital and produce a unique ID, we can now talk about building trees of hashes. We call these Merkle Trees. Just like a sports bracket, pairs of hashes can be hashed together, in a repeated fashion until you have only one hash, what we call the Merkle Root. Now here is the magic: Just like I could track a team through a tournament bracket and only need its opponents to see it progress to the winning slot, all I need is the hashes as they are combined to reconstruct the Merkle Root from the hash of an artifact. A proof that some data has not changed can be very small, even if it is only one of billions of entries in the beginning.

Lastly, a public witness is critical to the security of a Blockchain. Bitcoin uses a system of difficult hashing problems and a global network to ensure that all nodes in the Bitcoin network have the same, validated ledger. In fact, Bitcoin's ledger is certainly the most secure data structure on the planet. Including a Merkle Root into Bitcoin allows all of Bitcoin's security to be applied to truly huge sets of data.

Factom uses these basic concepts to allow its users to create their own groups of entries. Every 10 minutes the Factom Protocol writes one of these Merkle Roots of all the data collected into Bitcoin. This serves to "Anchor" Factom to Bitcoin. As a result, any modification to any part of Factom would "break" the

Factom Anchor. Factom will place anchors in many Blockchains, both public and private. Doing so makes the same Merkle Root available in many contexts. Syncing two systems based on different Blockchain or traditional systems only requires matching the latest hash. This allows an application running on a Private Chain to be able to run the same cryptographic proof as an application running on a different Private Chain.

Effectively applications can share process histories, transactions, market data, sensor data, product tracking, or any other data of interest.

It may seem very complex, these "Blockchains" and "Merkel Roots" and "Hashed Artifacts". One might ask, "What does a Blockchain solution bring to a problem that is radically new and different from existing solutions?"

The surprising answer is nothing new and different. But a much better solution.

Blockchains provide three things, accountability for the data entered, notification services of new data, and algorithms for ensuring all systems have the same data, i.e. consensus between systems.

We have solutions for accountability, notification, and consensus today. However, the older solutions are more error prone, more expensive, and complex to maintain. Blockchain based solutions hold the promise of deploying faster, accountable, lightweight solutions where the older approaches have failed.

Blockchain based systems will be able to track any manner of manifests and business processes for consumer goods, components, drugs, and food to ensure safety and quality. We will see Intellectual Property and Copyrights documented managed over Blockchain applications to streamline royalty payments and accelerate innovations. Increasingly mortgages are traded and move across different systems. Blockchain based solutions can and will ensure that such transfers do not lose data and result in the kinds of errors and mismanagement we saw in 2008 to 2010. Blockchain solutions promise to address issues in all sectors public and private, and address pain points in all industries. While we have had solutions in the past that sort of worked, Blockchain based solutions promise very disruptive changes that will bring greater efficiencies, transparency, privacy, and most importantly, accountability to all parties.

Mr. BURGESS. Yes. Not likely. Mr. Beccia, you are recognized for 5 minutes, please. The Chair thanks the gentleman.

Mr. Beccia is recognized.

STATEMENT OF JOHN BECCIA

Mr. BECCIA. Thank you, Chairman Burgess, Ranking Member Schakowsky, and members of the subcommittee. My name is John Beccia, and I am General Counsel and Chief Compliance Officer for Circle Internet Financial. We are a consumer company focused on making payments more secure, safe, and simple.

Circle is a member of the Electronic Transactions Association, the leading trade association for the payments industry. I am grateful to be part of the subcommittee's Disrupter Series. The blockchain represents one of the most important technical innovations of our time. It has potential to impact myriad industries, retail, media, health care, Government, and energy, but today I am going to focus, really, on how the blockchain can impact financial services, talk a little bit about the benefits, risks, and the regulatory environment.

There is no question that payments can be improved. Traditional payments are controlled by networks that charge fees for transactions and have cumbersome processes that are subject to data breaches. Digital currency holds promise to improve payments, since there is no central authority and the value is stored across a distributed network.

So what are the benefits? For consumers, it can be used in a variety of transactions. It can be used to split a lunch tab with your coworkers, a mother sending funds to a daughter in college, or someone sending money to a relative overseas. Digital currency makes these transactions simple, less costly, and secure, and it also provides instant access to funds. It also offers privacy, because on the blockchain personal information is not disseminated.

Digital currency has the ability to reach unbanked and underserved communities. Cross-border transactions are offered at a fraction of the cost of typical remittance fees. Merchants also like this technology because of the benefits. It is not subject to interchange fees, chargeback risks, or the liability of storing customer information.

Blockchain technology is still in its infancy. While there are over 12 million people with digital wallets, more than 100,000 merchants accepting Bitcoin, and nearly 200,000 daily transactions, the majority of consumers are still learning about the benefits of Bitcoin. Like any other technology on the Internet, adoption is going to take some time.

At Circle, we believe that money should be exchanged freely, the same way people exchange other information over the Internet, whether it is photos, messages, et cetera. Our social payments application allows consumers to make payments in multiple currencies on the Circle platform and to anyone anywhere in the world on the blockchain. It also is done in a fun mobile experience that uses tools like GIFs, emojis, and photos.

Incubation and blockchain testing among firms of all sizes is really setting the stage for the expansion of financial products, economic growth, and job creation. Now, there are some risks associated with digital currency, and I am sure you have heard about those risks, and the industry has worked very diligently to address those risks.

First, digital currency is subject to money laundering. Unfortunately, global AML laws are updated and really should be revised to account for 21st century technology. The transparent nature of the blockchain, however, provides us some more transparency to detect illicit activity. The industry has created risk management systems which are really innovative and have collaborated quite a bit with Government to address these risks.

Second, which I believe is important to this committee, consumer education and protection is vital. The CFPB and the FTC have issued advisories on digital currency. Companies in this space should have disclosures to provide clear language about fees, risks, obligations, and dispute resolutions. Consumers need to know their funds are secure, and that is why our customers have FDIC insurance protection if they are holding dollars in their account, and we have also secured private insurance for those customers who are holding digital assets.

Third, those digital assets really need to be protected, so companies like us who are acting as custodians need to have best-in-class protocols to ensure that we are protecting digital assets whether they are online or offline. And that is why we support the White House's recently announced Cyber Security Action Plan and feel that companies should work to make sure that all financial transactions are safe.

The regulatory environment for digital currency has evolved quite a bit over the last couple years. For companies like Circle, we need to be registered as a money transmitter at the Federal level as well as licensed State by State. Whereas States like California have pending legislation on digital currency, New York has created their own BitLicense, and that was finalized last year.

We are currently the one and only company that does have a BitLicense, and we take that responsibility very seriously. In addition, the Conference of State Bank Supervisors are coming out with regulatory principles, or have come out with principles, in an attempt to provide clarity among the States.

While we are encouraged by the regulatory framework, there is work to be done. Regulatory uncertainty and/or regulatory arbitrage makes it difficult for businesses to utilize this service and for consumers to feel confident in the service. We also encourage Congress to consider more efficient charter choices, both the digital currency-based firms as well as FinTech firms in general.

Disruption in payments is happening now. The lessons learned from digital currency and financial services can be applied to other industries, and we look forward to discussing that with you in question and answers.

Mr. Chairman, this concludes my testimony. I look forward to answering any questions you may have. Thank you.

[The prepared statement of Mr. Beccia follows:]

Testimony of
John Beccia
General Counsel and Chief Compliance Officer, Circle Internet Financial

Before the Commerce, Manufacturing and Trade Subcommittee of the House
Energy & Commerce Committee
U.S. House of Representatives

Digital Currency and Blockchain Technology

March 16, 2016

Introduction

Chairman Burgess, Ranking Member Schakowsky and members of the Committee, my name is John Beccia, and I am the General Counsel and Chief Compliance Officer of Circle Internet Financial, a consumer Internet company focused on transforming the world economy with secure, simple, and less costly technology for storing and using money. Circle is a member of the Electronic Transactions Association (ETA), the leading trade association for the payments industry, representing 500 companies worldwide who offer electronic transaction processing products and services.

I am grateful to be part of the Subcommittee's disrupter series and appreciate your efforts to examine the blockchain and its numerous applications. When it comes to technology like the blockchain, I believe this a pivotal moment that could lead to significant developments for several areas of commerce. The blockchain represents one of the most important technical and economic innovations of our time that could benefit businesses and individuals around the globe.

So what is the blockchain, exactly? The blockchain is a decentralized ledger of transactions that can be used to secure and validate any exchange of data, including assets, such as commodities or currencies. It offers multiple possibilities as it can be applied to any type of business transaction. It has the potential to impact myriad industries, such as real estate, media, hospitality, retail, life sciences, healthcare, government, and energy. As a result of the numerous applications, the world's largest companies have established working groups and dedicated significant resources to investigate how it can be used. Today, I will be focusing my comments on how the blockchain can impact financial services through digital currency.

56

The Blockchain's Impact on Financial Markets

There's no question that the existing payment system can be improved. In 2013, the Federal Reserve issued a report outlining payment trends and deficiencies and later created task forces to examine how to improve the speed, safety and efficiency of the U.S. payment system.[1] The traditional payment system is a hub and spoke model in which a single institution, such as a bank, acts as the hub and disseminates information. The movement of value is controlled by closed networks that charge fees for transactions and have a cumbersome process that is subject to data breaches and privacy leaks.

Luckily, we have seen a dramatic shift in financial services over the last several years with the development of new payment products, many of which were created by ETA members. Today, there are better choices to send and receive convenient, cost effective and timely payments, such as mobile applications, prepaid cards and P2P networks. Digital currency and the blockchain hold promise to further improve payments by lowering costs for businesses, decreasing fraud risk for consumers and merchants, increasing consumer privacy and protection, and expanding the market for financial products on a worldwide basis. With digital currency, there is no central authority or gatekeeper. Instead, account value is stored across the distributed network of computers. Like other open protocols that power the global Internet, the blockchain would make the exchange of value ubiquitous and free - the same way that people can now share information over the Internet today.

Benefits of Digital Currency

Digital currency has the ability to transform, both everyday payments and the wider economic outlook. For consumers, it can be used for a wide variety of transactions, such as co-workers splitting a lunch tab, a mom sending her freshman daughter grocery money, friends chipping in for a shower gift or businessman sending money to a relative overseas. In terms of benefits, digital currency makes these transactions simple and offers lower fees and instant access to funds in multiple currencies. It offers privacy and security as transactions on the blockchain do not involve dissemination of personal financial information that is later subject to identity theft or data breaches. While some question the anonymity component of the blockchain, it actually offers a real opportunity

---

[1] The 2013 Federal Reserve Payments Study Recent and Long-Term Payment Trends in the United States: 2003 – 2012 Summary Report and Initial Data Release Research Sponsored by the Federal Reserve System, December 19, 2013 and Strategies for Improving the U.S. Payment System, Federal Reserve System, January 26, 2015 (fedpaymentsimprovement.org)

to create new identity management tools that could benefit consumers. Digital currency has the ability to reach underserved and unbanked communities and radically expand access to financial services on a worldwide basis. Not only are these transactions instant and secure, they are offered at a fraction of the costs of remittance fees, which average 7.7% worldwide for cross-border payments.[2]

Merchants enjoy several attractive benefits as digital currency transactions are not subject to interchange fees, chargeback risks and the liability of storing personal customer information. This is especially beneficial to small business owners who may shun certain forms of payment due to high fees and risks associated with these transactions.

Blockchain technology is still in its infancy. While there are over 12 million people with digital wallets, more than 100,000 merchants accepting Bitcoin and nearly 200,000 daily Bitcoin transactions, the majority of consumers are still learning about the benefits and some have questions about the risks.[3] The users are early adopters, those seeking financial privacy and those who see Bitcoin as an asset rather than a currency. Like other technologies and innovations built on the Internet, adoption will take time as the technology improves, regulatory and policy issues are addressed and users become comfortable with the products and services. However, it is clear that a strong infrastructure has been created and digital currency will have staying power as it addresses needs among multiple demographics. For example, millennials seek a different way to send, store and receive money. In fact, 33% of millennials in the U.S. do not have a desire to interface with traditional banks and 70% feel that the payments system will be vastly different in five years[4]. As consumers' behaviors change, so must the technology and businesses that provide these services.

The Role of Start-ups in Payments Innovation

Venture capitalists have invested almost $1 billion in early stage companies that seek to promote the benefits of digital currency. These businesses include exchanges, wallet providers, payment processors and other financial vehicles.

---

[2] IMF Staff Discussion Note: Virtual Currencies and Beyond Initial Considerations, Dong He, Karl Habermeier, Ross Leckow,Vikram Haksar, Yasmin Almeida, Mikari Kashima,Nadim Kyriakos-Saad, Hiroko Oura,Tahsin Saadi Sedik, Natalia Stetsenko, and Concepcion Verdugo-Yepes, January 2016
[3] Coindesk, State of Bitcoin and the Blockchain, January 28, 2016
[4] See www.millenialdisruptionindex.com, Scratch Viacom Media Networks

Circle is one of the companies trying to alter the payments landscape. We believe money should be exchanged the same way people exchange messages, photos, content and other information over the Internet. Circle enables people to send money to anyone anywhere anytime with simplicity, speed, security, and no fees. Circle offers a social payments app that allows users to make payments in local currency, P2P payments across currencies that are on the Circle platform and payments to anyone anywhere in the world using the blockchain. This is done in fun mobile application experience that integrates social media and other messaging tools like GIFs, photos and emojis. Unlike other closed systems and networks, because companies like Circle utilize the blockchain for payments to individuals and merchants, customers have the ability to send payments freely to anyone across the globe.

It is not just start-ups and venture capitalists interested in this technology. A group of 42 of the world's largest banks formed a group called R3 CEV, which is actively testing the blockchain and its applications to legacy systems and the existing financial structure. They have several pilot programs in development and recently announced a trial testing for the trading of fixed income assets on the blockchain.[5] Members of the ETA are similarly, looking at ways to tap into this technology and apply it to their business.

Incubation among both smaller firms and global banks is setting the stage for the expansion of financial products, future economic growth and job development as burgeoning industries emerge. Jobs are being created for engineers, data scientists, compliance and risk professionals, finance staff and marketing personnel who are becoming experts in a new field. There is also a substantial infrastructure being built through vendors and professional services that are supporting this industry.

Risks and Innovations in Risk Management

The risks of digital currency have been well documented. The European Banking Agency (EBA) July 2014 report outlines over 70 risks associated with digital currency ranging from risks to users, risks to non-user market participants, risks to financial integrity, risks to existing payment systems, and risks to regulatory authorities.[6] To date, the majority of the policy discussions have involved four key areas: financial crimes risks, consumer protection, security and taxation. While these risks can't be ignored, the benefits of digital currency outweigh the potential downside and each of one of the risks can be properly mitigated with effective regulatory regimes and industry best practices.

---

[5] See R3cev.com press release dated March 3, 2016
[6] European Banking Authority Opinion on 'Virtual Currencies', July 4, 2014

Financial Crimes

Like other financial products, digital currency is subject to money laundering and related risks. The most notable case is Silk Road, which was a dark web site where bitcoin was used to purchase illegal goods and services before being shut down by the FBI. As regulated entities, companies like Circle are required to maintain an anti-money laundering compliance program that includes Know Your Customer (KYC) procedures, transaction monitoring of client activity and regulatory reporting of suspicious activity. We partner closely with U.S. and international law enforcement to investigate illegal use of digital currency and participate in working groups such as the Bank Secrecy Act Advisory Group (BSAAG), Blockchain Alliance and Europol's European Cybercrime Centre (EC3).

Unfortunately, portions of the Bank Secrecy Act and global anti-money laundering laws are outdated and should be revisited and revised to account for 21st century technology. If the goal is to "follow the money" and catch bad actors, we need to move beyond collecting data on individuals or filing reports and keeping records based on arbitrary currency amounts. The transparent nature of the blockchain offers the ability to detect illicit activity. We have developed risk management protocols and use forensic tools that provide insight into transactions on the blockchain. As a result, we collect more robust data that can be shared with law enforcement. Risk engines created by digital currency companies like ours could be a model for regulators, law enforcement and other traditional financial services firms.

Consumer protection

With the emergence of any nascent industry, especially those that handle customer funds, consumer education and protection should be at the forefront. Consumers will want to understand these products and know that the transactions are secure. The Consumer Financial Protection Bureau (CFPB) and the Federal Trade Commission (FTC) have issued consumer advisories warning about fees, price volatility, and issues relating to merchant transactions with digital currencies.[7] Both agencies have been collecting complaints from consumers who are using digital currency. We expect that the agencies may require further disclosures around these products in the future. In the meantime, companies should have detailed user agreements and transaction details that provide clear and conspicuous language about fees, risks, consumer obligations

---

[7] CFPB Bulletin, Risks to consumers posed by virtual currencies, August 2014 and FTC Consumer Information Blog Posted title, Before Paying with Bitcoins Kristin Cohen, June 22, 2015.

and dispute resolution procedures. Consumers need to need to know their funds are secure, which is one reason our customers holding U.S. dollars in their accounts have FDIC protection. We have also secured private insurance to protect against theft of digital assets for 100% our customers' funds.

Security

Digital currency price fluctuations can be volatile and digital assets must be secured properly to avoid theft. We saw this play out with the infamous loss of 750,000 Bitcoin at a Japanese digital currency exchange called Mt. Gox. These risks underscore the need to ensure digital assets are free from cybersecurity attacks, social engineering and other potential scams that could cause customers to lose funds. Industry members that act as custodians for digital assets need to take that responsibility seriously. The industry has responded by creating best in class protocols to secure online and offline digital assets, which offer multiple layers of protection and redundancies. We support the White House's recently announced Cybersecurity Action Plan[8] and believe that as digital currency matures, companies in this space need to develop ways to ensure financial transactions are secure and work closely with traditional and emerging payment companies in an effort to accomplish this same goal.

Taxation

Most countries, including the U.S., have determined that digital currency is property (or an asset) rather than currency and require reporting of gains and losses of these transactions.[9] Today's reporting and recordkeeping requirements are somewhat difficult and may negatively impact everyday usage. Also, because digital currency transactions are anonymous and involve the movement of high value across borders this creates potential tax evasion risks and reporting difficulties for business and consumers. While there are complexities for end users, the blockchain could transform financial audits and accounting by providing for more reliable, transparent and real-time financial reviews.

All of the risks discussed here are real, but not insurmountable. These risks are not creating barriers, but should instead be a catalyst for positive changes to legacy risk management techniques and archaic laws and regulations.

Payment Regulation - Past, Present and Future

---

[8] https://www.whitehouse.gov/the-press-office/2016/02/09/fact-sheet-cybersecurity-national-action-plan.
[9] See https://www.irs.gov/uac/Newsroom/IRS-Virtual-Currency-Guidance.

The regulatory environment for digital currency has changed dramatically over the last couple of years. It has moved from a position of fear and uncertainty to an embracing of the possibilities. The advent of digital currency has created unprecedented coordination with regulatory agencies, law enforcement and industry in an effort to further understand the benefits and risks of this technology.

Circle has been thoroughly engaged on regulatory issues since the company began operations. We want to educate governments and be transparent as we enter new markets and seek regulatory approvals. We have coordinated and testified before key state and federal government agencies in the U.S. and abroad and believe that a certain level of regulation is needed to promote stability and consumer confidence. Regulations should focus on activities that pose the highest risk and should be measured and allow innovation to develop.

Development of the Current Regulatory Environment

The pivotal marker for regulation came in March 2013, when the Financial Crimes Enforcement Network (FinCEN) issued guidance that firms which exchange digital currency for fiat currency must register as a money service business (MSB) and implement a formal anti-money laundering program.[10] On the state level, similar companies need to be licensed as money transmitter on a state-by-state basis. This is a more onerous process since states have different requirements and most current state statutes do not account for digital currency. While some larger states like California have pending legislation to deal with digital currency specifically[11], the New York Department of Financial Services (NYDFS) issued the first ever BitLicense in 2015.[12] The BitLicense offers similar consumer protections as money transmission laws, but also takes into account risks and reporting considerations specific to digital currency. Circle is the first (and currently only) company to receive a BitLicense. In addition to the BitLicense, the Conference of State Bank Supervisors (CSBS) has issued principles for a regulatory framework in attempt to provide consistency and clarity among the states and combat the current unwieldy licenses and oversight process for money transmitters. [13]

---

[10] US Department of the Treasury, Financial Crimes and Enforcement Network, "Application of FinCEN's Regulations to Persons Administering, Exchanging, or Using Virtual Currencies" (Guidance FIN-2013- G001, March 18, 2013).

[11] See https://leginfo.legislature.ca.gov/faces/billNavClient.xhtml?bill_id=201520160AB1326.

[12] See NYDFS Regulations on Virutal Currencies at
http://www.dfs.ny.gov/legal/regulations/adoptions/dfsp200t.pdf.

[13] Conference of State Bank Supervisors, State Regulatory Requirements for Vitrtual Currency Activities CSBS Model Regulatory Framework 10, (Sep. 2015).

From a global perspective, European jurisdictions had been slow to adopt digital currency regulations following the EBA report, however recently the UK Treasury has announced they are working on new guidance and UK regulators are accepting e-money applications for digital currency firms[14]. The EU Commission has focused on issuing new guidance to address the money laundering risks as part of the Fourth Money Laundering Directive. In addition, Japanese and Canadian regulators have issued positive statements regarding new regulations that will not interfere with the development of this technology. And, central banks in England and China have voiced a desire to issue government backed digital currency and review how the blockchain could impact monetary policy in the long-term.

Future Regulatory Innovation

While we are encouraged by the regulatory framework that has developed to date, there is still work to be done. Some jurisdictions are still skeptical of digital currency and have varying degrees of guidance. Regulatory uncertainty makes it difficult for businesses to operate and consumers to have confidence in the system. In addition, we need consistent regulations. Any level of regulatory arbitrage, whether between U.S. states or from an international perspective will increase risks and not allow the technology to flourish. We would like to see continued innovation in the regulatory space. The convergence of new Internet-based methods of savings and lending, new digital currency-based payment services, and potential government-issued digital currency should lead to the development of new forms of "Internet Bank Charters" that define the rules and requirements of operating a global digital bank that uses fundamentally new methods of intermediating financial risk. We are encouraged that federal financial regulators, like the Office of the Comptroller of the Currency (OCC), have created a working group to "develop a framework to evaluate new and innovative financial products and services".[15] We encourage Congress to consider more efficient charter choices and regulations for these industries.

Conclusion

The Comptroller of the Currency, Thomas Curry, stated it best when he noted that "new payment systems are creating greater efficiencies and convenience, and virtual

---

[14] See HM Treasury report titled, Banking for the 21st Century: Driving Competition and Choice, March 2015.
[15] Thomas J. Curry Comptroller of the Currency Before the Federal Home Loan Bank of Chicago Chicago, Illinois August 7, 2015.

currencies offer the prospect of instantaneous transactions directly between individuals and entities on a global basis". He further stated that "these innovations are potentially revolutionary in their impact, and are advancing at a breakneck speed."[16] Digital currency offers the ability move money freely at low cost in safe and secure manner to a variety of users. This type of innovation should be encouraged and embraced. While there are risks associated with digital currency, these risks can be addressed by the industry and regulators. Governments should resist the temptation to overreact to risks or external events. We believe a bold and balanced approach toward oversight on behalf of lawmakers is paramount to success of digital currency.

Disruption in payments is happening right now. The lessons learned from digital currency's use of the blockchain will ultimately help shape exciting advancements for other industries. Innovations like smart contracts that are self-executing and able to verify when certain conditions are met, or a blockchain-based property ownership recordkeeping system that can reduce costs and fraud in the real estate market are just some examples of what the future holds.

Mr. Chairman, that concludes my prepared testimony. On behalf of Circle and the the ETA, I appreciate the opportunity to appear before you. I would be happy to answer any questions for the Committee.

---

[16] Remarks by Thomas J. Curry Comptroller of the Currency Before the Institute of International Bankers Washington, D.C., March 2, 2015.

64

Mr. BURGESS. The Chair thanks the gentleman.
Mr. Syracuse, you are recognized for 5 minutes.

STATEMENT OF DANA V. SYRACUSE

Mr. SYRACUSE. Mr. Chairman, Ranking Member Schakowsky, I thank you for inviting me here to speak today. My name is Dana Syracuse. I am counsel at BuckleySandler LLP, and I am the former Associate General Counsel of the New York State Department of Financial Services, which is the principal financial services regulator in New York State.

While I was there, I was responsible for helping to lead several initiatives, including bringing enforcement matters against some banking institutions for AML/BSA failures and violations of OFAC sanctions programs, helping to lead the department's effort in the area of cybersecurity, and also helping to lead the department's efforts in the area of regulation of emerging payment systems, including Bitcoin, blockchain, and my current practice at BuckleySandler focuses on these same areas.

For the sake of clarity, I want to break out what the regulatory environment looks like in the area of the payment system around Bitcoin, separate and apart from blockchain. I agree with my fellow panelists that the Bitcoin payment system really is revolutionary and has the power to bring into the financial fold the unbanked, the underbanked, and those who may not have the benefit of a modern banking system.

It also has the possibility of being the catalyst of driving the modernization of our Apollo era payment system into one that is faster, less expensive, and more reliable. But the challenges faced by regulators in this new era is going to be how to create the appropriate guard rails that protect consumers, prevent money laundering, and impose proper cybersecurity standards while at the same time not hindering innovation.

In New York, with the drafting of the BitLicense, where we came out was not regulating Bitcoin, not regulating the underlying blockchain protocol, but rather taking a functional approach and regulating those who are acting as financial intermediaries, meaning those who are put, in essence, in a position of trust. So that includes the law companies, exchangers, and transmitters.

And because of the kinds of functionality that they were offering, the regulation, therefore, imposes certain capitalization requirements, anti-money laundering requirements, cybersecurity, which I think the importance of cannot be understated, and the other challenge is how to do this while at the same time continuing to help foster innovation.

And that is why the BitLicense has an on ramp for smaller companies, and it is something that I would encourage any other States or regulatory bodies that choose to step into this area also include, because the fact of the matter is, you know, this is an area that has a tremendous amount of innovation, and it is, I believe, unreasonable and could be a hindrance to innovation to potentially saddle companies like that without outsized compliance functions that may not necessarily equate with the potential dangers that are there.

I also believe that a uniform approach would—across all the States would be a good goal. The Uniform Law Commission has an effort underway right now, and Mr. Beccia mentioned the CSBS model framework as another example.

Now, turning to blockchain, you know, there is—the blockchain is the underpinning backbone architecture on which different applications can be built, Bitcoin being the most well-known. There is significant interest in the way banks and clearinghouses and exchanges may use blockchain to transform existing business models, whether they be through closed systems or on the public blockchain.

Significant time and money is being spent in understanding this. While blockchain is new, the kinds of functionalities that are going to come out of it—securities clearing, identity management—those are not. So the question that needs to be asked is, you know, when these new functionalities arise, is there an existing regulatory framework that already answers the question or meets the concerns, if it is for protection concerns, the AML concerns, that Government and regulators could potentially have.

The other important thing to take away from this is that regulation around the blockchain protocol itself would be a hindrance to innovation. It is ill understood right now, companies that are doing some of the creative work in there haven't reached I would call it market adoption yet sufficient to say that it is worth the candle of potentially saddling them with burdens that they don't need.

In conclusion, you know, regulation in the area needs to be smart. It needs to be the result of study. And I thank you and look forward to your questions.

[The prepared statement of Mr. Syracuse follows:]

Dana V. Syracuse
Counsel, BuckleySandler LLP
Former Associate General Counsel
New York State Department of Financial Services

Congress of the United States
House of Representatives
Committee on Energy and Commerce
Subcommittee on Commerce, Manufacturing, and Trade

Disrupter Series: Digital Currency and Blockchain Technology
Washington, D.C.
March 16, 2016

My name is Dana Syracuse and I am Counsel at BuckleySandler LLP. I appreciate this opportunity to present testimony before this Subcommittee and thank Chairman Burgess, Ranking Member Schakowsky, and the Members of this Subcommittee for their hard work in organizing this public hearing.

Up until this past August I was Associate General Counsel at the New York State Department of Financial Services. NYDFS regulates and supervises the activities of nearly 1,700 insurance companies with assets exceeding $4 trillion, nearly 300 state chartered banks with assets of $2.1 trillion, and more than 1,600 licensed financial entities. While I was with NYDFS, I was responsible for several initiatives including enforcement activities in the area of AML/BSA compliance, helping to lead our efforts in the area of cyber security, and helping lead the Department's initiative to regulate emerging payment systems including digital currency and Blockchain technologies, and the creation of the BitLicense regulation. My current practice at BuckleySandler focuses on these same areas.

Regulation of Digital Currency

State Level

For the sake of clarity, and because they are two very different things, I'd like to first discuss digital currency regulation and then move onto a discussion of Blockchain technology.

Digital currency, in the form of Bitcoin or other open-source crypto protocol, is both (i) a form of value and (ii) a mechanism to transfer such value allowing a nearly instant peer to peer payment system without the need for a financial intermediary. This revolutionary payment system has the potential to bring into the financial fold the unbanked and the underbanked, and allows one to send money to any part of the world without the benefit of a modern banking system. It is noteworthy that the global mobile penetration has been reported at 73% through 2014. This continuum of mobile adoption combined with the advent of digital currency are the catalysts driving modernization of our Apollo era payment system into one that is faster, safer, less expensive, and more reliable. The challenge faced by regulators in this new era will be how to create appropriate guard rails that protect consumers, prevent money laundering, and impose proper cyber security standards while not hindering innovation.

In the summer of 2013 New York launched an initiative to understand Bitcoin, other digital currencies, and the Blockchain. The initiative included a first in the nation two day hearing similar to the hearing we are in today; meetings with countless industry representatives, academics, attorneys, and members of the law enforcement community; consultation with regulators at the State, Federal, and International level; the issuance of two proposed regulatory frameworks; and the review of over 3,700 public comments. There were many commenters with the opinion that digital currencies should not be regulated as the cost of doing so would collapse this innovative and growing industry. There were however, equally as many on the other side of

68

the coin if you will, that wanted a regulatory framework to create a legal basis to operate and a structure for compliance. This fairly lengthy process and debate led to the final Bitlicense regulation issued in July 2015.

The regulatory approach we took in New York was a functional one. We started with the premise that digital currency had monetary value and didn't debate whether it was "money" or "currency" as defined under current law. We focused on the "activity" – i.e., exchanging, transmitting, selling, holding value, rather than on how to best classify the value. This meant not regulating Bitcoin, the underlying digital currency, or the Blockchain technology, but rather the licensure of those that are acting as financial intermediaries or are providing financial services to the public. Based on the voluminous feedback from the industry, our goal was draft a tailored regulation to only capture entities performing services associated with administrative, custody and exchange of the value and not regulate individual use or the underlying technology itself. Additionally, we also believed that a sound regulatory framework would also need to include key provisions to safeguard customer assets, which should include requiring capitalization to allow for sufficient funds on an ongoing basis and in the event of a wind down; consumer protections to guard against fraud and abuse; controls to prevent money laundering and other illicit activity, including examinations, anti-money laundering compliance, accounting and recordkeeping; and cyber security controls. The core concept is that entities that are providing these types of services are entrusted with safeguarding customer assets and, in exchange for receiving a license to do so, accept heightened regulatory scrutiny.

We also learned that regulators also must to be very sensitive to the need to innovate. This means that any act that seeks to regulate this type of financial services functionality must also create a permissive environment where smaller companies can innovate. There is much debate as to whether this should be in the form of a tiered license structure, such as in New York, or in the form of a safe harbor that exempts smaller entities from licensure. In either instance, this requires an analysis of whether smaller players present a risk and whether that risk warrants the kind of regulatory structure that may be better suited to regulating a larger player. Every effort should be made to ensure that small companies who do not present a great risk to consumers are not required to implement outsized compliance programs that put them at financial risk.

Of equal importance is an understanding of who is not providing financial services or products, and should therefore not be regulated. This includes:

- Individual use of digital currency. If an individual chooses to use digital currency in a criminal enterprise that is the act that should receive legal oversight, not the fact that it was effectuated using Bitcoin.

- Non-financial use of this technology.

- Those who create software for the use of others and are not otherwise engaged in providing financial services.

Other States including California, Connecticut, Georgia, Kansas, New Hampshire, New Jersey, North Carolina, Pennsylvania, Tennessee, Texas, and Wyoming either have or are in the process of establishing their own regulatory frameworks either through existing money transmitter law or new frameworks specifically crafted for the this type of regulation. There are also efforts underway to promote uniformity among the state regulations by the Conference of State Banking Supervisors and the Uniform Law Commission. These frameworks also promote a functional approach. One last point worth making, which state's and the uniform law efforts are considering, is the need for some type of regulatory reciprocity from state to state. The internet is borderless. Jurisdictional lines are easily crossed or blurred. People travel easily from one state to the next or one country to another and transact business. Which jurisdiction's rules should control? A fifty state regime with different requirements is a costly and time consuming venture to set up. It would be in the best interest of the regulators to consider how best to regulate various industries in the electronic age in order to foster innovation and efficiency and at the same time address needed consumer protections.

Federal Level

Since 2013 the Financial Crimes Enforcement Network has required that those in the business of virtual currency exchange to file as Money Service Businesses and meet certain compliance obligations around anti-money laundering. In May of last year FinCEN announced that it was in the process of conducting audits of those who had registered with them and that it had reached a settlement with a digital currency company who had failed to file Suspicious Activity Reports and maintain an adequate anti-money laundering program. Digital currency is also on the Consumer Financial Protection Bureau's radar. In August 2014 the CFPB issued a warning about the risks posed by digital currencies including cost, potential loss from hackers, and the fact that consumers may have fewer redress rights when dealing with custodians of virtual currency. Both FinCEN and the CFPB's approaches are of note because, like NYDFS, they also are taking a functional and/or activity based approach to oversight. Similar approaches can be seen in enforcement matters brought by the Securities and Exchange Commission and the Commodity Futures Trade Commission. Late last year in an enforcement action against a bitcoin mining company and its principal, the SEC ruled that mining contracts can be contracts and therefore were securities regulated under the Securities Act and were therefore within the SEC's jurisdiction. In September 2015, the CFTC announced a civil enforcement action against a bitcoin options platform. This action confirmed that if bitcoin is acting like a commodity or being used like a commodity it will be regulated as such.

Regulation of Blockchain Technology

The Blockchain provides the underpinning backbone architecture on which different applications can be built – bitcoin being the most well-known. There is significant interest in the way banks, clearinghouses, and exchanges may use Blockchain to transform existing business models, whether through closed proprietary systems or on the public Blockchain, and through the use of smart contracts and electronic agents. Significant time and money is being devoted to understanding things like reducing latency in businesses and in doing so lessening counterparty and settlement risk, not to mention cyber security. Others are attempting to use Blockchain technology for services may traditionally be unregulated.

These technologies are in their infancy and beg two questions 1) are they governed by existing regulatory frameworks, and 2) is new regulation needed to regulate the underlying Blockchain protocol itself? If a function or activity that can be performed by the Blockchain has not been traditionally regulated it may not be necessary to burden it with undue regulation simply because it is effectuated through the Blockchain. To the extent that there is an existing framework in place, such as in the world of financial services, then that may be sufficient for the time being. That being said, just because a transaction is effectuated through the Blockchain does not mean that rights that were once there should be stripped away because it has been automated through a smart contract. The core concept is that though the Blockchain is a new technology the types of value and asset transfer that it permits are not. Existing frameworks, such anti-money laundering provisions, may be sufficient though regulators also need to consider issues that arise as a result of utilizing the Blockchain to effectuate transactions, such as transparency and cyber security. The importance of a sound data privacy and cyber security program cannot be understated. Entities that are leveraging the benefits of the Blockchain and companies that are regulated under digital currency regulations exist almost entirely in a digital environment. Therefore, they must be sensitive to the safety and soundness issues that poor cyber programs may create. As for regulation of the underlying protocol, it's simply too early to act. Most of the relevant projects haven't garnered enough clients to make them viable business models and are ill understood by those outside their respective working groups. As pointed out by the European Securities and Markets Authority it is exceedingly difficult to regulate a decentralized ledger, like the Blockchain, that has no physical owner. The only alternative would be to regulate through the code itself which at this stage may only serve to stifle innovation.

Conclusion

In conclusion, we are in exciting times. Technological innovation is driving true constructive change in commerce, payments and financial services. Business processes are being redefined. It's not so much about Bitcoin per se as a competing currency, but rather Bitcoin and the Blockchain as a wedge between the past and the future –a disrupter to the current payment and asset exchange systems and as a mechanism to force industries to use technology to increase speed, accuracy, and reduce friction and costs. Regulatory frameworks can provide the necessary support to facilitate investment and growth. A functional, uniform, and reciprocal approach to regulation that is tailored to the risks posed and will act to set up guardrails that both allow the technology to flourish and protect the consumer at the same time. The states and federal agencies thus far have taken a thoughtful functional approach to regulating digital currency. The various use cases for the Blockchain, whether for clearing and settlement, supply chain, title transfer, smarting contracting, medical records, etc. are still in their infancy and need time to develop and mature unencumbered.

Thank you for your attention, for organizing this hearing, and for providing me with the chance to discuss these important issues. I will be happy to address any questions that you may have.

Mr. BURGESS. The Chair thanks the gentleman.

Mr. Roszak, you are recognized for 5 minutes for an opening statement, please.

STATEMENT OF MATTHEW ROSZAK

Mr. ROSZAK. Good morning, and thank you, Chairman Burgess and the distinguished subcommittee for the invitation to testify today. I would also like to commend your staff for the thoughtful engagement going into today's hearing.

My name is Matthew Roszak, and I am pleased to be here on behalf of the Chamber of Digital Commerce where I serve as chairman. The Chamber is the world's largest trade association representing the blockchain industry. Through education, advocacy, and working closely with policymakers, regulators, and industry, our goal is to develop a pro-growth legal environment that foster innovation, jobs, and investment.

I am from Chicago, and I have been working as a venture capitalist and technology entrepreneur for 20 years, deploying over a billion dollars of capital and founding a dozen companies during my career. I have also invested in over 20 blockchain companies through my firm, Tally Capital, and more recently I co-founded a software company called Bloq, with Jeff Garzik, a technology visionary and core developer of Bitcoin.

Blockchain technology has captured the imagination of thousands of innovators around the world and created what I call a generational opportunity for entrepreneurs and investors. That translates into once in a lifetime. So think railroads, automobiles, telephony, and the Internet. It has the potential to play on that scale or even greater. From the recent covers of the economists and Bloomberg, if it feels like you are reading about blockchain everywhere, well, it is because you are, and there is a good reason for that.

The technology of money has evolved over the centuries from shells, wampum, salt, tally sticks, gold, and paper currency, to bits and bytes. Today banking and finance are in the process of being redefined as blockchain technology is creating an entirely new operating system for money and poised to be one of the most important inventions in the history of finance.

Trusted intermediaries will soon be disrupted and decentralized peer-to-peer networks will blossom reducing tons of friction and saving billions in transaction costs while unlocking financial access to the entire world, yet we are still in the early days akin to the dial-up phase of the Internet.

In terms of Bitcoin's State of the Union, and taking a famous quote from Charles Dickens' A Tale of Two Cities, "It was the best of times, it was the worst of times." This very much applies to Bitcoin today. Despite some of the sensational headlines, investment and innovation in this industry has grown at an incredible pace. Venture capital surpassed a billion dollars last year, with some of the best and brightest entrepreneurs and professionals from Silicon Valley to Wall Street to K Street all racing in, along with over 100,000 merchants accepting Bitcoin for goods and services.

Bitcoin is indeed alive and well. And also named companies, such as Citibank, Deloitte, Foxconn, IBM, PwC, Microsoft, NASDAQ, and many more have all dedicated significant resources to exploring blockchain technology.

I would also like to highlight a challenge the Bitcoin community is currently facing. Something tells me this committee might be able to relate. Making decisions in a decentralized system is not easy. Bitcoin is experiencing significant growing pains as the num-ber of transactions are increasing exponentially. This is a clear in-dicator of Bitcoin's success and a testament to its global adoption. Now, the challenges reside in how to best increase the through-put of the system in order to support greater transaction volumes. Unlike a Government or company, there are no members of Con-gress in Bitcoin, nor a CEO or board. That is all purpose-built and part of the fundamental power and beauty of Bitcoin's math-based composition.

However, when there is friction in decision-making, that gridlock can sometimes be overwhelming, if the debates, fights, and pas-sions involved are in many ways a feature of the system and not a bug. There is an opportunity on the horizon to create an open forum for building consensus with more constructive ways to out-line goals, priorities, and risks, which would serve as an important barometer for stakeholders in the ecosystem. And there are plenty of well-known platforms to draw from, including W3C, ICANN, Wikipedia, Linux, and even the United Nations, where certain best practices can be explored and leveraged.

Extremely talented and brilliant people have solved some of Bitcoin's toughest problems. These statesmen usually work as vol-unteers, purely out of love for the technology. Through their Hercu-lean efforts, the system's features, security, and especially its resil-ience have all improved dramatically. The system stresses, heals, learns, and evolves.

In conclusion, the amount of financial and intellectual capital being poured into this ecosystem, I see incredible promise and op-portunity, especially with hundreds of startups betting their lives on blockchain, and believe this new technological frontier has the potential to benefit society and industry with privacy, security, and the freedom of conveyance of data, which in my mind ranks up there with life, liberty, and the pursuit of happiness.

Thank you very much.

[The prepared statement of Mr. Roszak follows:]

Written Statement by:

MATTHEW ROSZAK

Chairman, Chamber of Digital Commerce

Co-Founder, Bloq, Inc.

Prepared for:

COMMITTEE ON ENERGY AND COMMERCE
OF THE UNITED STATES HOUSE OF REPRESENTATIVES

Subcommittee on Commerce, Manufacturing, and Trade

"Disrupter Series: Digital Currency and Blockchain"

March 16, 2016 | Washington, DC

INTRODUCTION

Good morning and thank you Chairman Burgess and the entire Subcommittee for the invitation to testify today about digital currencies and blockchain technology. I would also like to take this opportunity to commend your staff for the thoughtful engagement and preparation going into today's hearing.

My name is Matthew Roszak and I am very pleased to be here on behalf of the Chamber of Digital Commerce, where I serve as Chairman. The Chamber is the world's largest trade association representing the digital asset and blockchain industry. Our mission is to promote the acceptance and use of digital assets and blockchain-based technologies. Through education, advocacy, and working closely with policymakers, regulatory agencies and industry, our goal is to develop a pro-growth legal environment that fosters innovation, jobs and investment. Our membership is open to all those investing in and innovating with blockchain technology and is composed of the key blockchain companies, global technology firms, and financial institutions.

I'm from Chicago, Illinois, and have been working as a venture capitalist and technology entrepreneur for 20 years – and have invested over a $1 billion of capital, and founded a dozen companies during my career. Over the last 3 years, I have invested in over 20 companies in the digital currency and blockchain industry through my investment firm, Tally Capital – and more recently, I co-founded a blockchain enterprise software company called Bloq with Jeff Garzik, a technology visionary and core developer of bitcoin. Bloq enables leading companies to scale their blockchain platforms with supported software and services.

In only a few short years, a technology that began as an alternative digital currency has captured the imaginations of thousands of innovators around the globe, and has created a generational opportunity for entrepreneurs and investors – that translates into *once in a lifetime* – think railroads, automobiles, telephony and the Internet – it has the potential to play on that scale, or even greater. This potential and sharing these perspectives is why I am here to testify today.

From the recent covers of the Economist[1] and Bloomberg[2], if it feels like you're reading about blockchain technology everywhere, well it's because you are – and there's a good reason for that.

Blockchain technology is one of the most important inventions in the history of finance – and the functions of many middlemen will soon get disrupted – and decentralized, peer-to-peer networks will move in, to reduce tons of friction and save billions in transaction costs, while unlocking incredible financial access and personal privacy to the world.

New products and services derived from blockchain technology have the potential to revolutionize entire categories of industry – including banking, government records, title and asset ownership, digitization of and encryption of medical records, digital identity, trading, clearing and settlement, secure voting systems, and many others.

---

[1] *The Promise of the Blockchain*, The Economist (Oct. 31, 2015)
http://www.economist.com/news/leaders/21677198-technology-behind-bitcoin-could-transform-how-economy-works-trust-machine

[2] Edward Robinson and Matthew Leising, *Blythe Masters Tells Banks the Blockchain Changes Everything* (Aug. 31, 2015) http://www.bloomberg.com/news/features/2015-09-01/blythe-masters-tells-banks-the-blockchain-changes-everything

Digital currencies allow for money to be programmable. With bitcoin, the world's smartest and most creative software developers have an open platform on which to build products and services that will allow individuals, businesses, governments and even machines to do business with each other more efficiently and productively.

The blockchain is a newly created medium of and platform for money (or anything of value for that matter). Money has been redefined in the past -- from bricks of salt, to cowry shells, to wampum, to tally sticks – the utility of paper money will soon go away. Today, banking and finance are again in the process of being completely redefined. Digital currencies and blockchain technology create an entirely new operating system for money.

Not only is all of this a technological marvel, but it has also become the start of an impactful social movement for individuals, industries and governments.

WHAT IS BITCOIN AND WHAT IS THE BLOCKCHAIN?

When we talk about bitcoin, it is important to make a distinction between bitcoin the currency and the blockchain. While most of the discussions, hearings and debates (and the often sensational press coverage) among regulators, innovators, and public policymakers regarding bitcoin have focused on its use as a digital currency, some of the greatest potential for bitcoin does not lie in its use as a currency, it lies within the blockchain.

The blockchain is a peer-to-peer digital asset transfer system that is independent of any third-party intermediary, including financial institutions and governments. In short, it is open-source software that is available to the public. Anyone and everyone may have access to it and innovate with it.

The first blockchain application was bitcoin the digital currency and is still what most people think of today when they think of bitcoin. What makes the bitcoin digital currency so unique is that it is based entirely on mathematics. In other words, no longer do consumers need to rely on a financial institution to settle transactions, the settlement process is integrated into the software network, via complex math verification features, making sending money instant, globally accessible, and extremely cost-effective.

Bitcoins can be bought from exchanges, ATMs or from other users. Bitcoin users are assigned a unique encrypted identity and can conduct transactions with other users that are recorded on a public ledger (i.e., blockchain) and are visible to computers on the network, but does not reveal any personal information about the parties to the transaction.

The blockchain holds a radically transparent, public ledger of all bitcoin transactions. It also verifies and authenticates these transactions. In addition, anyone may independently audit the transactions.

Bitcoin would not have happened without open source, and the transparency associated with it. Engineers and early enthusiasts could read the source code for themselves. Adopters did not have to trust Satoshi (bitcoin's creator) – just trusted the math, not the man. There are no hidden pieces of the puzzle with open source software.

Open source creates more secure, trusted software through peer review, just like biology or chemistry or another science. Bitcoin and blockchain technology is trusted because it has been widely reviewed by cryptography experts as well as battle tested in the field for years.

Open networks spur permissionless innovation, which creates a vibrant, fast-paced technology community that promises a more secure, more transparent world.

THE INTERNET AND THE BLOCKCHAIN

We are still very early in the evolution of digital currencies and blockchain technology – akin to the dial-up phase of the early Internet

Blockchain technology possesses many of the same attributes as the Internet. It is an open and global infrastructure upon which many other technologies and applications can be built upon. The Internet is used to connect people and send information around the world instantly.

However, sending anything of value over the Internet is an issue developers have been working on for decades, as the process was very susceptible to hacks, attacks, double spending, criminals, and other issues.

The invention of the blockchain's decentralized, cryptographically secured, public ledger is a technological leap in computer science allowing anyone to send anything of value or to establish an immutable record over the Internet instantly, efficiently, securely, and without the need for a trusted third-party intermediary.

On the horizon we are going to combine the Internet of information with the Internet of money -- these two things compound each other – the Internet as we know it is great for collaboration and communication, but deeply flawed when it comes to commerce and privacy – blockchain technology fixes that – which means loans without banks, contracts without lawyers, and stocks without brokers, executed and recorded across hundreds of servers at all corners of the earth.

Some things are hard to explain, or understand, until you experience them. In 1994, *The Today Show* ran a small discussion of a new technology called "The Internet". It did not go well as Katie Couric thought that the "@" symbol stood for "about" – and they eventually had to ask a producer off-camera "what Internet is.[3]"

By the way, the 1994 Internet had 2,700 web pages, compared to today's Internet with over 1 billion web pages.

BITCOIN'S STATE OF THE UNION

Taking a famous quote from Charles Dickens' book, *A Tail of Two Cities:* "It was the best of times, it was the worst of times..." – this very much applies to bitcoin today.

Bitcoin has certainly had its share of negative PR – between SilkRoad and Mt. Gox – to price volatility, wallet hacks and ransomware – however the tide has turned dramatically over the last couple of years.

Investment in and innovation on the blockchain, since the publication of the original Bitcoin Whitepaper[4] in 2008, has grown exponentially. Venture investment has eclipsed $1 billion in

---

[3] The Today Show. "Flashback! The Internet in 1995 | Archives" YouTube (Jun. 13, 2014) https://www.youtube.com/watch?v=95-yZ-31j9A

[4] Satoshi Nakamoto. "Bitcoin: A Peer-to-Peer Electronic Cash System." (Nov. 2008) https://bitcoin.org/bitcoin.pdf

the past year[5], some of the best and brightest from Silicon Valley to Wall Street to K Street are all racing into the industry, along with over 100,000 merchants now accepting digital currency for their goods and services.

Prominent financial institutions and technology companies including Bank of America, Citi, Deloitte, Foxconn, Goldman Sachs, IBM, Intel, PwC, Microsoft, NASDAQ, Samsung, UBS, and many more have dedicated significant resources to study, experiment, and innovate with blockchain technology.

Over 50 household name global banks have publically announced their respective blockchain initiatives, Wall Street is now marching to the beat of the blockchain drum. So are banks on the brink, or on the offensive? A report from Santander InnoVentures[6] estimates that blockchain technology would yield over $20 billion in annual costs savings for banks by 2022.

Historically, banks have had a love-hate relationship with technology going back to the early days of the Internet and even Y2K, mobile proliferation and then having their systems pressure tested during the 2008 financial crisis. Today, banks don't face competition by other banks, but by the developer sitting in Silicon Valley. The unbundling of financial services is playing out in front of our eyes – starting with companies like PayPal, to today's challengers like Lending Club, Square and Venmo – all of which will only be further magnified with the proliferation of blockchain enabled payment rails.

---

[5] CoinDesk. Bitcoin Venture Capital Report. http://www.coindesk.com/bitcoin-venture-capital/

[6] Mariano Belinky, Emmet Rennick and Andrew Veitch. *"The Fintech 2.0 Paper: rebooting financial services."* Santander InnoVentures http://santanderinnoventures.com/wp-content/uploads/2015/06/The-Fintech-2-0-Paper.pdf

DEBATE IS A FEATURE, NOT A BUG

Bitcoin is a car going down the road at 1,000 mph. Developers are not the drivers of this car, yet they are tasked with repairing and upgrading this car without turning it off, stopping it or rebooting it.

I'd like to discuss a challenge the Bitcoin community is currently facing – something tells me this Committee might be able to relate.

Making decisions in a decentralized system is not easy — the bitcoin ecosystem is currently facing some significant growing pains as the number of transactions has been growing exponentially — over 200,000 transaction per day. This is a clear measure of success and a testament to bitcoin's adoption and evolution. The current challenges reside in finding a path forward on how to increase the throughput of the system, and drive more transactions to support the growth of this platform.

Unlike a government or corporation, there are no "Members of Congress" in Bitcoin, nor a CEO or board of directors. That is all purposeful and part of the fundamental power and beauty of Bitcoin's math-based system. However when there is friction in the system on a particular topic, the gridlock can be overwhelming. It is a bit like trying to change the rules to "rocks-paper-scissors."

Furthermore, the current challenges do not really reside in any specific technical component. Instead, the issues reside in the human factor of communication, and finding a way of building consensus during the early days of this $6.5 billion railway. The debates, fights and passions involved are in many ways a feature and not a bug of the network.

There's an opportunity on the horizon to create a more robust forum for discussion, debate and consensus building — with clearer ways to outline goals, priorities and risks involved in any particular scaling path moving forward. This discussion forum could act like a barometer for various stakeholders, which ultimately vote on which scaling path to run on their systems.

There are several well-known examples of sharing ideas and driving consensus, even with your greatest competitor or your worst enemy. Some of these platforms include W3C, ICANN, Wikipedia, Linux, and even the United Nations — a subset of the best practices utilized by these organizations could be leveraged and applied to Bitcoin.

Any healthy community will draw on the strength of its members. Bitcoin has done this to a degree which is, frankly, astounding. It is living proof that, when people are dedicated to a common cause, the best and brightest ideas will rise to the top. Extremely talented and brilliant people have solved some of Bitcoin's toughest problems. These "statesmen" usually work for free, as volunteers, purely out of a love of the technology.

Through their efforts, the systems' features, security and resilience have all improved dramatically. Problems are identified and solved. Bitcoin learns, and heals; it reacts to stresses and it evolves.

But, as it grows, it faces governance challenges which it is currently struggling to overcome. These challenges, I would imagine, are similar to those faced by the US Congress on a daily basis. This industry needs a *call to action* to resolve its differences and find a path forward.

CONCLUSION

Digital currency and blockchain technology is an important emerging area that has the potential to transform the financial services industry, and beyond. An October 2015 Congressional Research Service (CRS) report[7] cites three potential benefits of bitcoin: 1) Lower transaction costs for electronic economic exchanges; 2) Increased privacy; and 3) No erosion of purchasing power by inflation. These benefits continue to increase as the number of bitcoin users and businesses entering the digital currency market grows. These factors will call for greater oversight of the industry not just by federal agencies but by Congress as well. Additionally, states are now starting to weigh in through legislation and regulation. Congress could play an important role by establishing uniform standards that could preempt conflicting state laws and provide greater clarity to the industry and its stakeholders.

Given the amount of financial and intellectual capital being poured into this ecosystem, I see great promise in blockchain technology – and that development will require cooperation among industry, technologists and regulators – an open dialogue with policymakers is a critical ingredient to this industry's long term success.

---

[7] "Bitcoin: Questions, Answers, and Analysis of Legal Issues." Congressional Research Service (October 13, 2015) https://www.fas.org/sgp/crs/misc/R43339.pdf

However government does not move at the speed of innovation and there needs to be a balanced approach applied as to not impair investment flows, job creation and innovation. There are currently over 1,000 startups betting their lives on blockchain-enabled technologies. Applying light touch regulation – similar to the UK, Singapore and Canada – with a "wait and see attitude" (much like the early Internet) will create jobs for Americans and help keep innovation in the United States.

In conclusion, I believe digital currencies and blockchain technology have the potential to benefit society with privacy, security and freedom of conveyance of data — which in my mind, ranks up there with life, liberty and the pursuit of happiness.

Thank you, and I look forward taking questions and discussing these topics further with you.

Mr. BURGESS. The Chair thanks the gentleman and thanks all of our witnesses. We will move into the Q&A part of the hearing. Each member will have 5 minutes, and we will go one round and perhaps longer. We may have a series of votes that interrupts us, but let me recognize myself for 5 minutes.

Mr. Syracuse, very fascinating testimony from all of you, but yesterday a situation was brought to my attention where someone was—a crime was committed, and the crime was committed using something called ransomware, which I did not know about until yesterday. It is a fairly interesting technology that I guess criminals have developed, and the payment was instructed to be made in Bitcoins.

Now, it wasn't like a bag of Bitcoins be taken down to the wharf and left under a boat. It was, you know, where do you go with this stuff? And when I questioned, you know, "Well, why don't you just follow the digital trail?" he was like, "You can't do that." So can you kind of enlighten me and the subcommittee on what are saw of the law enforcement aspects here?

Mr. SYRACUSE. Sure. I mean, I think that there are a couple of things going on in that story. You know, firstly, virtual currency, Bitcoin, it is highly traceable. There are services in place that regulators and law enforcement have and need to educate themselves of if this is going to be regulated that allow one to follow using blockchain forensics, the flow of funds from one exchange to another or from wallet to wallet.

The issue also is, at a certain point, that person is going to need to exit and get Fiat out. So that speaks to the importance of making sure that the exchanges—the entry points and the exit points, the on ramp and off ramp—are regulated. And also, that story, it is less about virtual currency and Bitcoin.

You know, Bitcoin is used as cash, which can be used in criminal enterprise. They kind of outlawed that, but it is a story about cybersecurity, and a larger conversation that needs to be had around regulation in that area and creating proper standards there.

Mr. BURGESS. You know, maybe I have watched too many crime dramas on TV, but it seems like Clint Eastwood would have put an ink cartridge into the bag of money that stained the dollar bills, so that anyone knew when they were pushed across the counter that this guy is the criminal. Is there any way technologically to attach that sort of detection device to the Bitcoin transaction?

Mr. SYRACUSE. I think that there are coins that are known now that have been used in criminal enterprises that are, in essence, marked. But, yes, they can be programmed in such a way. But the key thing is to make sure that these blockchain forensic tools are being utilized, so you could follow it, so you could trace the funds.

Mr. BURGESS. Well, you know, again, that was interesting. That case just literally came before me yesterday as we were preparing for this hearing today.

Mr. Brito, did you have something you wanted to add to that? Mr. BRITO. Sure. One thing to keep in mind about ransomware, which is a very serious problem, is that it predates Bitcoin and decentralized digital currencies. We have seen ransomware as far back as 20 years, and what makes ransomware possible today is three things.

It is a breach of a computer. Essentially, you get hacked. Number two, cryptography. Essentially, your files on your computer aren't encrypted, so you no longer have access to them. And, number three, it is a payment method. So in this case it is Bitcoin. So you can pay the person who is in ransom.

Of those three things that are necessary for ransomware, encryption and digital currencies have incredible potential, you know, good uses, right? So cryptography is what keeps our bank balances safe. Digital currency, as we have talked, is what makes it possible.

The third component, though, the breach, the hack, the lack of cybersecurity, that is where the real concern is. And I am happy to say that, in conjunction with the CDC, Coin Center and a lot of the companies in this space have created something called blocktion lines, which is a public-private forum between law enforcement and the companies in this space to begin to discuss and educate law enforcement about how they can do this kind of tracking to, you know, get the bad guys.

Mr. BURGESS. Are there places a criminal can go, countries to which they can go, where these traceability aspects are muted or disrupted?

Mr. BRITO. So the traceability of the coins, as it were, on the network cannot be compromised. You can still trace the coins. The problem is that the off ramp and on ramp may be in a country that is not cooperating with law enforcement in other countries. But that, again, is an issue not of Bitcoin's issue, of cooperation between law enforcement.

Mr. BURGESS. Mr. Suarez, just briefly let me ask you, how do you determine the value of a Bitcoin? Is it all one unit size, or are there various sizes?

Mr. SUAREZ. Well, the value of Bitcoin is determined in the same way that the value of really any kind of digital asset or commodity is determined, which is effectively through supply and demand. And so the price of Bitcoin on the coin-based platform today, which is probably something in the low $400 range, is really just a function of how many people are willing to purchase Bitcoin and how many people are willing to sell it.

To your question about fractions of a Bitcoin, the reality is you can transfer fractions of a Bitcoin, very tiny fractions of a Bitcoin, just as easily as you can a full Bitcoin, or many Bitcoin. And that opens up very exciting possibilities.

So, for example, one of the issues I think that was discussed today is the concept of micro payments online where I can viably send you two pennies worth of value or 10 pennies or 50 cents worth of value because I am going to tip you because I like a comment that you made on my Internet form, for example. And that is not a technology or that is not a payment form that is viable today, because the cost of those smaller payments would exceed the value of that transfer. So we can transact in tiny fractions of a Bitcoin.

Mr. BURGESS. That is very interesting.

The Chair recognizes Ms. Schakowsky of Illinois, 5 minutes for questions.

Ms. SCHAKOWSKY. Thank you, Mr. Chairman. I apologize for being late. I did get to hear most of the testimony.

I wanted to ask questions about consumer protection also and financial fraud and abuse. There is all kinds of protections set up to guard against financial fraud and abuse through traditional currency transactions. Banks can flag suspicious activity and limit withdrawals, which make it harder for a thief or a fraudster to empty out our bank accounts.

And I understand that those kinds of checks may not be in place for digital currency, but I did—and another example would be that the consumer protections required by the Truth in Lending Act may not apply to loans or credits of digital currency, raising questions about transparency and about fairness.

So, Mr. Syracuse, I wanted to ask you, you have experience in the public sector and in this kind of regulation. If a consumer needs to contest a purchase made, for example, with Bitcoin, say the product they bought is defective or the service was never performed, are they protected in the same ways that they would have been if they had used a credit card or a debit card?

Mr. SYRACUSE. Not necessarily. But depending on what exchange or what facilitator they are using, they may have those policies in place. You know, I would be curious to—the answer is not necessarily.

Ms. SCHAKOWSKY. Not necessarily. And are those kinds of risks, then, disclosed? Do consumers——

Mr. SYRACUSE. Yes.

Ms. SCHAKOWSKY [continuing]. Make assumptions, do you think?

Mr. SYRACUSE. Yes. So under the BitLicense, there are certain enumerated disclosures that need to be made. So disclosures about volatility, disclosures about the irreversibility of a transaction, they have to be made.

Ms. SCHAKOWSKY. And in what form—you know, I get all of these privacy disclosures and all of these things that just say "punch agree" if you agree?

Mr. SYRACUSE. Well, that is the issue is at what point does one kind of turn a blind eye to it? And then the other issue is, in this digital environment, you know, how much information can one actually absorb in that little screen? You know, I think that there should be a conversation around what consumer protection looks like in the digital age as our banking functions shift from brick and mortar to an increasingly mobile environment. I think it is going to be kind of a necessary area to roll up our sleeves.

Ms. SCHAKOWSKY. And what are those things, other ways that the digital currency exchanges and wallets can be better protected, and what would that look like? Sure. Mr. Snow, sure, and then Mr.——

Mr. SNOW. I would like to change the conversation just a little bit, because it is in fact true that digital currency is—what am I trying to say? Nonreversible, yes. It is a nonreversible transaction. But blockchains do have the potential for the consumer to have a much more assured understanding of what they are purchasing.

So let me tell a really short story about a friend of mine who builds computer parts on a sideline. He is retired, so now he spends hours and hours in a bedroom building little kits. It is what intel engineers do, I guess.

And one of his parts, if it is not an authentic part, the whole board that he creates, bricks, it kills itself. And he can work at it, beat on it, and bring it back to life, but his customers get really upset if it has a nonauthentic part on his board. So he bought a bunch of chips from Alibaba, you know, the Chinese eBay sort of thing, and they assured him he was getting valid chips. And he put them on the board, and they weren't valid.

And then when he goes to their consumer protection group, the manufacturer always wins. Therefore, he just had to go find some more parts and replace all these chips.

Now, here is where the blockchain can help you. Because you can create a public notified ledger of where parts came from, the manufacturer of the real genuine part could have put on a chain, "These are parts I have sold to Company X." And Company X could put on that same chain that it sold these parts to Company Y.

And then Company Y could be the guy that my engineer friend is talking to, and he says, "I want authentic parts," and they say, "Yes, you have these three parts. And, see, they are in this chain, and I can cryptographically prove that there is a path of legitimate parts that came from the manufacturer to this guy, and he is about to sell them to me."

Now, others would say, "Well, he could turn around and still send you the bogus parts, right?" But, see, the trick is, when the next customer said, "Sell me some parts," Company Y would have already said, "He sold the legitimate parts to my friend." He would have to represent the real parts as clones.

And so you are in a position where we can create audit trails for consumers that exist in places well beyond our jurisdictions to prove that when you are buying goods and services, drugs, food, that it is coming from where it is stated that it is coming from, and limit the ability of middlemen to pass off clones and knockoffs as the real product.

Now, that doesn't help at the refund level.

Ms. SCHAKOWSKY. I am going to—we are going to—we are about to——

Mr. SNOW. It does help to——

Ms. SCHAKOWSKY [continuing]. Get a gavel here, because we have gone over time. So I hear you saying, though, that you can—we can build into the creations of consumer protections, but I am not convinced that we don't need some assurances, outside regulations, some sort of framework that we all agree to, and I think the conversation, unfortunately, can't continue now.

But I think that is the conversation we need. How do we do it? And maybe some of it is embedded and some of it is imposed.

Thank you.

Mr. BURGESS. The gentlelady yields back. The Chair thanks the gentlelady.

Mr. Lance, 5 minutes for questions.

Mr. LANCE. Thank you, Mr. Chairman.

What privacy concerns should the public consider when the public is thinking about buying digital currency? To the panel in general, anyone who would like to respond. Yes.

Mr. BECCIA. So I would just note there is a couple of things that come up in terms of privacy in digital currency. First, there is a lot of questions about the anonymity of digital currency, and, you know, digital currency does offer benefits to consumers. It offers financial privacy.

So when you are doing a digital currency or Bitcoin transaction, you are not giving over your credit card information or your personal information in that transaction. So if you are buying something on a merchant that accepts Bitcoin, like at Overstock.com, that is just a cryptographic type of code that you are providing them and not that personal information.

So it is actually a benefit in terms of from a consumer perspective. But on the flip side, where regulators look at it and are concerned as far as the anonymity, and so not understanding either where that money is going or who that customer is. And so what we kind of do to mitigate the risks are, obviously, similar to any other financial service, we have to really know who our customers are.

And so we have detailed AML programs, and we look at the unique risks of our customers. Our customers are mostly online customers. They are customers from multiple countries, and they are conducting digital currency transactions, which are a little more complex. So we need to create systems that are a little more technically advanced to address that.

Mr. LANCE. Thank you. At the moment, the public can invest in gold or silver or currencies. Does the public have the ability to invest in these digital currencies? Yes?

Mr. SUAREZ. Yes, Congressman. So absolutely. So one of—the platform we operate, for example, will allow customers to establish a coin-based account, indicate how many Bitcoin they want to purchase, and then to send us money to settle a purchase transaction.

And so the simple answer to your question is, yes, there is an existing retail platform that allows customers to purchase Bitcoin.

Mr. LANCE. And the price fluctuates, I presume, as is true of any other currency?

Mr. SUAREZ. That is exactly right. And so most of our customers today, at least at Coinbase in the United States, are attracted to the volatility of Bitcoin, because they are investing effectively in an asset whose value they anticipate will go up. And so a lot of savings energy is being poured into that.

Obviously, there are many more applications of virtual currency beyond that, but that is the initial use that we see.

Mr. LANCE. Thank you. Are there differences between a public blockchain and a private blockchain? Mr. Cuomo?

Mr. CUOMO. Yes, I will take that one. So I think when we typically think about blockchain, we associate Bitcoin. But the interesting thing is that the blockchain is a design pattern that can be applied very broadly.

And when we start to apply it to managed things of value—that can be land deeds, any kind of certificates, birth certificates, death certificates, contracts—things that are managed by, let's say, regulated environments, it is attractive to start thinking about a blockchain that is permissioned. All right? Not just anonymous, right?

And the beautiful part about the blockchain architecture is it allows for this. And the way I am thinking about it is a dial, right, where you can dial in at one level very tight permissions, so think about it as a membership club. To get in, you have to at the door show them your ID card and you are allowed to come into the room and transact.

But a permissioned blockchain could also be permissive, right? You can open it up and be somewhat liberal. For example, two parties exchanging carve-in numbers may have a certain level of permission to exchange cars with one another. Maybe one is an auto manufacturer; maybe the other is an auto dealer.

But the Department of Motor Vehicle—and you might only be able to see those cars that pertain to you, right? So you will have permission to only see the things on the blockchain that are relevant to your transactions. But the Department of Motor Vehicle, when it came in through the door of the club, of the car club so to speak, it was given broader permissions as an auditor in that blockchain network. So it can see more, and it can actually be able to provide an auditing service.

Mr. LANCE. Thank you. I certainly know who IBM is, BuckleySandler. These other entities, are these new to our commerce in this country? Bloq? Factom? Coinbase? Are these relatively new organizations?

Mr. SNOW. We are a really, really old blockchain company of about 2 years.

Mr. LANCE. I see.

Mr. SNOW. It is a very new space. Most of us are fairly new.

Mr. LANCE. I see. Thank you. My time has expired.

Thank you, Mr. Chairman.

Mr. BURGESS. The gentleman yields back. The Chair thanks the gentleman and recognizes the gentleman from Florida, Mr. Bilirakis, 5 minutes for questions, please.

Mr. BILIRAKIS. Thank you, Mr. Chairman. Appreciate it so very much. Thanks for holding the hearing as well.

Mr. Roszak, many have raised concerns regarding the potential for terrorism financing due to the ability of users to make anonymous transactions. Address that, please.

Mr. ROSZAK. Criminals——

Mr. BILIRAKIS. Address the concerns, yes.

Mr. ROSZAK. Yes. Criminals have always been early adopters of the newest technology, whether that goes back to the days of NASCAR and having a faster car or cell phones or the Internet or, in this case, digital currencies being used for terror finance and money laundering.

As we have heard on this panel, the traceability of digital currencies is more and more profound. The Chamber of Digital Commerce co-founded the Blockchain Alliance, and we are working with law enforcement to help them provide the forensics and tracing for certain issues that come about with those use cases. But those are the very fringe use cases, and, quite frankly, digital currencies, es-

94

pecially Bitcoin, is not a great use of funding for criminal activities like that.

Mr. BILIRAKIS. Thank you. Anyone else wish to address that? Yes, please. We will go here—down here.

Mr. BRITO. Sure. I would add that to date we have not seen terrorist financing using digital currency, although it absolutely is a possibility. What we see instead is the use of prepaid cards and other centralized methods that can truly guarantee anonymity, and we see the Director of the Financial Crimes Enforcement Network at the Treasury Department testify before Congress in a hearing about digital currency that cash is still the number one way that folks launder money and conduct terrorist financing.

Mr. BILIRAKIS. Who else? Briefly, please.

Mr. SYRACUSE. I would also just add that, you know, it is probably more of a concern in the traditional banking environment. I know that when I was with New York DFS we brought major enforcement actions against banks for failing to follow sanctions programs.

And also, you know, to date, the virtual currency community, the Bitcoin community—the ones that are licensed have been very responsive, and the figure that I heard to date was that something like 5,000 suspicious activity reports had been filed. So to the extent that you are dealing with a regulated institution, hopefully it is capturing bad activity.

Mr. BILIRAKIS. Go ahead, please.

Mr. SNOW. One thing to understand is Bitcoin is a public ledger, and so the larger your organization is, the more transactions you have. The more transactions you have, the more ability forensics has to look at the blockchain and see the picture of your organization. This means that Bitcoin blockchain is decidedly a terrible use for large criminal organizations.

And this came out in the Department of Justice's digital currency conference that they had last year at the Federal Reserve Bank in San Francisco, and the FBI and numerous agencies stood up and said basically, "We can dig these organizations out of the blockchain. So we really would like them to use it. We can capture them."

I do think that individuals, small fry, might get through a lot easier with digital currency, but the larger the organization, the more opportunity to trip up and the more opportunity to catch them.

Mr. BILIRAKIS. Thank you very much. Very informative. Next question, again for Mr. Roszak, what advantages are there for consumers to utilize Bitcoin and other digital currencies, rather than traditional ways to send and receive assets today?

Mr. ROSZAK. Bitcoin, for example, is used for a variety of use cases, both as a currency and a store of value. From a currency standpoint, it could also be used for micro transactions. So think of a nickel going over the Internet is expensive today. Using Bitcoin or digital currencies, it is very cheap, very efficient, secure, and fast. And a nickel might not sound like much, but a nickel from 50 million people starts to add up. Part one.

Part two, remitting money around the world is a very expensive endeavor, time-consuming endeavor. Right now, the remittance industry is about a half a trillion dollars in size. That can get turned upside down with remittance saving lots of money and putting that back into the global economy.

Mr. BILIRAKIS. Thank you. Next question, why is the price of Bitcoin so volatile and is there fluctuation in purchasing Bitcoin? Or does fluctuation occur for the funds already purchased and available in a consumer's eWallet? I know that the chairman addressed this to a certain extent, asked this question, but yes.

Mr. ROSZAK. Fundamentally, Bitcoin is in a price discovery phase, and it is a supply and demand dynamic. And we are still in the early days of Bitcoin. There is 15 million, plus or minus, Bitcoins outstanding today. It has got a market value of about 400, so it is a $6 ½ billion currency today.

On a relative basis, that is small. But if you look at historically, it has been one of the better performing currencies on the plant. And as you have heard, the amount of investment and innovation that has been planted in this industry is still yet to be seen. And so we are at the front end of this.

Mr. BILIRAKIS. Thank you. You wish to——

Mr. BECCIA. I was just going to point out a similar thing, that it is a supply and demand issue. And it is a fact that, really, the users are using it or looking at it as early adopters more as an asset rather than a currency or a payment vehicle. And I think long term, as we see more people using it for payments, which I think is really the use case, we will see a greater stability in the price and we won't see as much volatility.

But in the meantime, I think that for consumers it is important for companies in this space to, one, educate consumers about the price volatility, and then do things to make sure that those risks are mitigated.

So as I mentioned earlier, for example, a company like Circle, we allow our users to also hold their value in U.S. dollars, which is not subject to volatility, but still have the benefits of making transactions on the blockchain. So there will be different innovations that will take out the price volatility, but I think long term, from an economic perspective, we will see less fluctuations.

Mr. ROSZAK. One final point in terms of financial access. So buying a cup of coffee or a pair of jeans here in DC with Bitcoin is not going to change our lives. But if you are a soccer mom in Brazil, a goat herder in Ghana, or a taxi driver in Indonesia, you have a super computer in your pocket, and you could buy Bitcoin, and that allows you to participate in the global economy. So financial access is a huge driver of digital currencies globally.

Mr. BILIRAKIS. Thank you very much.

Mr. BURGESS. The gentleman's time has expired.

The Chair recognizes the gentlelady from Illinois for redirection.

Ms. SCHAKOWSKY. Thank you. Mr. Syracuse, I wanted to ask you a couple more questions. In your testimony, you stated that regulators should focus on the uses of blockchain rather than their underlying technology. In New York, you led the process of developing the BitLicense program, as you stated in your testimony, and this process focused on the use of Bitcoin for digital currencies and included a two-day hearing with a wide range of stakeholders.

So what were some of the issues that were discussed in your hearing?

Mr. SYRACUSE. I think at the hearing there were discussions of, obviously, the technology, how does it work, the extent to which Bitcoin, the currency, should be regulated and what different aspects of the ecosystem should be regulated.

And the result of that was this kind of functional approach, which was figuring out what are the traditional functionalities that kind of fall within the jurisdiction, which would mean financial—those offering financial services and financial products.

Ms. SCHAKOWSKY. But were there existing laws that covered or—

Mr. SYRACUSE. No.

Ms. SCHAKOWSKY [continuing]. Could cover?

Mr. SYRACUSE. So this is another one of the debates which was whether or not to put virtual—to regulate this area under existing money transmission law or create something new. And where New York came out was that for our law, our New York State money transmission law, would only govern transmission of money from Point A to Point B and wouldn't capture the exchange companies or the wallet companies.

Now, that is not to say that other States would be able to capture that kind of functionality under their own money transmission laws.

Ms. SCHAKOWSKY. And have some of the other States been doing that or not?

Mr. SYRACUSE. Some other States are. Some other States are. So I believe North Carolina, New Hampshire, and a handful of others are attempting to do that. And that is a perfectly valid approach. Ms.

SCHAKOWSKY. What factors unique to digital currencies did the department think were important in developing new regulations?

Mr. SYRACUSE. Well, the way we initially kind of got interested in it was we were getting inquiries from our money—the money transmitters that we regulated saying, "Is this money? What should we do with it?" And then that kind of launched our inquiry. So we sent out subpoenas, we started meeting with numerous members from industry, law enforcement, academics, and the thing that was interesting was the way these new service providers were popping up in the ecosystem.

And then we started wrestling with, well, what are the anti-money laundering concerns? What are the consumer protection concerns? Cyber security, you know, the BitLicense weaves in a cybersecurity provision. New York State now is trying to lead the effort in having a nationwide conversation about regulation in cybersecurity. That is a very important factor.

Ms. SCHAKOWSKY. Absolutely. Mr. Beccia, earlier you seemed to want to make a point and didn't have time. I wondered if you wanted to say anything now.

Mr. BECCIA. I thought the consumer protection point was very important, and so just to give you a little more of a flavor of what companies in the space are looking at. I think, obviously, from a State standpoint, States like New York and others, and that are regulating this either as money transmission or from a separate licensing perspective, have right in their regulations very detailed consumer protection protocols, whether it is disclosures to marketing materials at the point of sale, dispute resolution, and whatnot. And so we are very, very cognizant of those.

I think also there is protections for customer funds, which are vital, and so every State—we have to segregate our customer funds, we have to have surety bonds for funds, and things like that.

At the Federal level, I think the CFPB and the FTC are very engaged here, and so they have issued warnings and advisories. They have started to collect complaints on their portals. And I would expect to see more regulations in terms of disclosures and things that are important and things that are—you know, you see at more traditional financial services and apply them to digital currency.

But I think, really, the big picture here is that, you know, we operate in a regulatory environment that is very similar to financial services. We are still the one and only company that has received a BitLicense, and so I can tell you, having gone through that process, it was almost like getting a bank charter. And so New York took a very thoughtful approach and was very thorough in terms of things that Mr. Syracuse mentioned, the very important risks, which are AML, consumer protection, and cybersecurity.

And so I think, you know, not only do we have those which are similar to financial services, but on top of that they are really dealing with the specific risks for this industry.

Ms. SCHAKOWSKY. Thank you. Thanks all of you.

Mr. BURGESS. The gentlelady yields back. The Chair thanks the gentlelady.

We do have a series of votes on, but I wonder if I could just go down the panel and ask for your thoughts on what is going to be the game changer that consumers see, what application of blockchain technology. Mr. Brito, we will start with you, and then we will just work down the line.

Mr. BRITO. Sure. I think if I knew, I would be out building it and making a fortune. So——

Mr. BURGESS. Wait a minute. Wait. You are not suggesting this isn't a productive use of your time.

Mr. BRITO. No.

Mr. BURGESS. Being in front of the United States Congress. Come on. This is where I live my life. Please proceed.

Mr. BRITO. That said, you know, as with the early Internet, I think the killer applications are going to come from left field, maybe things that we can't expect. But if I had to take a guess today, I would say it is going to be in areas where technology excels and does things that our current payment system and our current sort of asset systems do not do. And to me those are micro transactions and macro transactions.

So the ability to have very, very small payments that today our existing payment systems do not allow to be efficient or economic. Imagine, you know, if you think about the web, the business model of the web is essentially either charging you a monthly big fee, for video, for audio, for articles, or showing you advertising.

The only reason we have that choice of business models is because we can't pay directly a few pennies for this one article or this

98

5 minutes of audio. This technology for the first time makes it possible.

The other is macro transactions, really big cross-border payments that today are expensive and take a long time because of the expense and inefficiency in the corresponding banking system.

Mr. BURGESS. Mr. Suarez.

Mr. SUAREZ. Thanks, Mr. Chairman. That is a great question, and I also don't know the answer to that. But when I think about some of the core attributes of what substantialized virtual currency offers, for example, you can engage in a transaction without having to disclose your confidential payment credentials, and so there are security advantages there.

The cost—as Mr. Brito was just mentioning, it opens up opportunities for all sorts of micro transactions that are, you know, just economically not possible using credit cards. And you think about the global scale of this, which is like the Internet. Anyone can plug into it. Literally, anyone in the world can develop applications on top of the Bitcoin protocol. You start to appreciate the enormous potential.

So I think a lot of the opportunity lies in micro payments. There are people working on technology to allow micro payments in browser, and that is what Mr. Brito I think was getting at, where you can visit a Web page and automatically transact a micro payment to click through to read something rather than having to view ads or have a pay wall.

There are enormous potential, as my colleagues have discussed, in terms of using it as a clearance or property transfer mechanism. And so I am not sure which of those is going to take off, but it is going to be something I think very impactful.

Mr. BURGESS. Very well.

Mr. CUOMO.

Mr. CUOMO. Yes. Thanks for the question. Great question. You know, I think for every one payment, coin-oriented use case, there are thousands of nonpayment, noncoin-oriented use cases. So what really captures our imagination at IBM are some of the use cases that might happen around things like Internet of things where they intersect with everyday life.

So think about insurance and liability. Think about the new autonomous vehicles, self-parking vehicles out there. So who is liable if a self-parking vehicle crashes? All right? So I think what we can give back to our citizens is finer grain with the blockchain, finer grain liability insurance, such that when you are in control of the car, it is immutably recorded on the blockchain that you are in control, you are driving.

And when the software takes over in your car and starts parking, that is immutably placed on the ledger, such that if an accident occurs while, you know, the car is self-parking perhaps, the manufacturer is liable or the person who wrote the software. So when you start thinking beyond coins, you know, what the possibility is, it is just amazing.

Mr. BURGESS. Mr. Snow, and let's be brief because I have only got a couple minutes left before I have to go vote.

Mr. SNOW. Well, you are beginning to know me, because maybe I am not always brief. I do believe that the idea that you can know the history and the history can't be changed and you can distribute that to all corners of the earth will create new ways to organize projects and companies and efforts.

And so you will see a dramatic reduction in the overhead of corporate oversight essentially to create products, goods, and services to people. It is basically distribute everything, and what that looks like I will——

Mr. BURGESS. We will have to wait and see, won't we?

Mr. SNOW [continuing]. Like everyone else, I don't know.

Mr. BURGESS. Mr. Beccia.

Mr. BECCIA. Yes. So very quickly, thank you, Mr. Chairman. So when you think about the early days of the Internet and how long it takes for real innovation to evolve, I think you are going to see the same thing here, but it is really exciting. I think when you look at the payment space and you look at the risks, you look at the regulations that are needed, it is amazing where we have come even in a short period and where we can go.

But I am really also excited about the other use cases. So when you think of having real estate transactions, recordkeeping systems for those, for securities, for smart contracts, things like that, I think, you know, there is endless possibilities there.

Mr. BURGESS. Wonderful. Mr. Syracuse.

Mr. SYRACUSE. I think my fellow panelists have touched upon most of the salient points, exchanges, the ability in insurance, the ability in big data to put ownership of one's identity and credentials information into their own hands, so it is an asset that they are able to then leverage.

But I think the truth is, the people that know the answer to this question are probably sitting in a dorm room at MIT or a dorm room in another part of the world, and the key thing for us is to make sure that nothing that, you know, we do as regulators will prevent or hinder that, and will create an environment where that can grow.

Mr. BURGESS. Yes, Mr. Roszak.

Mr. ROSZAK. We have heard a lot of great use cases for the movement of money, digital currencies, tokenization of assets. And one of the greatest assets that can be employed into this new railroad is digital identity, how we manage that identity, the privacy, the security, and make each transaction unique, whether you are buying something at the convenience store or applying for a job or going to the hospital or applying for a mortgage.

Each of those interactions takes a different part of your digital identity, and this technology enables you to really take control of that and do that privately and securely.

Mr. BURGESS. Since the observation was made that someone in a dorm room right now is maybe working on that, whatever that next technology is, I will just offer that at some point in the future to have my individual medical records only accessible by me, but the larger, the identified data available to researchers, FDA, whoever wants to study the cross-hybridization between this medication and cardiovascular disease, the Vioxx story from several years ago might have been very, very apparent had that capability been available.

I want to thank all of you. You know, some mentioned the Internet of things. I have just got to tell you, when we had the Internet of things hearing, we had things here. When we had the drones hearing, we had drones here. I was so looking forward to finding out whose face was on the Bitcoin, and I still don't know even after the end of this hearing.

But seeing as there are no further members wishing to ask questions, I again want to thank our witnesses for being here.

Before we conclude, I would like to submit the following document for the record by unanimous consent: a letter from Ripple. Without objection, so ordered.

[The information appears at the conclusion of the hearing.]

And pursuant to committee rules, I remind members they have 10 business days to submit additional questions for the record. I ask our witnesses to submit their responses within 10 business days upon receipt of those questions.

Without objection, the subcommittee is adjourned.

[Whereupon, at 1:20 p.m., the subcommittee was adjourned.]

[Material submitted for inclusion in the record follows:]

PREPARED STATEMENT OF HON. FRED UPTON

Our Disrupter Series continues as we focus on digital currency and blockchain technology, just another example of how innovative uses of technology are powering the economy into the future. From executing smart contracts to settling money transfers in minutes instead of days, millions of folks in Michigan and across the country could see the blockchain transform how they engage in everyday commerce in the next few decades.

The exciting aspect about this technology, however, is that it can do much more than impact currency, it has the potential to affect almost every industry that relies on intermediaries to establish trust between two parties that want to do business. This can change how folks sell their car, sign a mortgage, or share music.

Back home in Michigan, startups are raising millions in venture capital to grow their blockchain-based businesses. For example, BTCS, headquartered in Troy, Michigan, raised $4.25 million in 2015 to develop its transaction verification services business on the Bitcoin blockchain.

In the manufacturing space, supply chain management continues to challenge companies' internal management functions as well as recall effectiveness. Given that the blockchain shows everyone in the network the current state of any asset and that asset's history on the blockchain, tracking a particular good around the world from port-to-port is now possible and the information trustworthy, which can help improve logistics for the auto industry.

In the public sector, blockchain technology could positively disrupt voting, compliance, and real-time reporting.

The applications for blockchain technology are truly incredible. Everywhere there is an asset transfer, the blockchain can bring transparency and trust. As with any emerging technology, it is important to understand the risks and benefits to consumers and I hope our panel can speak to these issues for digital currency and future blockchain applications.

I thank Chairman Burgess for continuing the Disrupter Series and highlighting the positive impact that emerging technologies, like the blockchain, are having on our economy.

⋅⁏ripple

March 14, 2016

Re: Disrupter Series: Digital Currency and Blockchain Technology

Chairman Upton and Members of the House Energy and Commerce Committee:

My name is Ryan Zagone, the Director of Regulatory Relations at Ripple, a technology company that delivers distributed technology (broadly referred to as "blockchain technology") to financial institutions. Ripple aims to enable a more transparent and efficient payment system, to reduce friction between currencies, and to broaden access to financial services.

I applaud the Committee for its leadership in exploring virtual currencies and blockchain technology and am grateful for the opportunity to submit this statement.

I write to highlight a pivotal shift in the application of these new technologies – from a direct-to-consumer offering within Bitcoin to an enterprise solution within the traditional financial services sector. The enterprise use of these tools takes advantage of their benefits, without creating consumer risk or the likelihood for misuse, as seen within Bitcoin.

With this shift to an enterprise tool in mind, this statement focuses on four themes:

1. **While Bitcoin was a technological breakthrough, it is not a realistic solution for financial infrastructure.** The underlying technology has evolved and is taking root as a tool within the financial services sector where consumer protections remain fully in tact.

2. **Public policy should recognize the various use cases of the technology.**

3. **A workable regulatory framework is needed to keep the United States competitive.**

4. **International coordination is key for effective policy.**

I thank you for considering my comments and am happy to assist with any questions.

Sincerely,

███████████

Ryan Zagone
Director of Regulatory Relations, Ripple
zagone@ripple.com

1

 268 Bush Street, #2724 · San Francisco, CA 94104

1. While Bitcoin was a breakthrough, enterprise use cases of blockchain technologies are taking root.

The development of Bitcoin – both the virtual currency and blockchain (the database that records transactions within the system) – were breakthroughs in payments technology. This new technology was initially applied in a direct-to-consumer model. Consumers directly engaged with the technology while assuming the risk of holding a volatile currency with no recourse in the event of a problem.

This model created a host of consumer protection concerns which have been the focus of regulatory attention to date. Further, "mining" – the process central to Bitcoin's operations – has proven highly inefficient and energy-intensive, requiring a dependency on unknown third parties that are concentrated in foreign and often sanctioned countries.

For these reasons, new approaches have emerged that leverage lessons from Bitcoin yet greatly improve upon the underlying technology. Often, it takes several iterations of a technological breakthrough before a realistic solution is developed and takes root.

Over the past year, there has been a shift from direct-to-consumer uses of the technology to enterprise approaches where traditional financial services firms leverage the tools for new products and improved services. The enterprise approach utilizes the benefits of the technology without creating consumer risk or other vulnerabilities.

Ripple is one such enterprise solution: it is a platform for financial institutions to facilitate real-time, cross-border payments on behalf of their customers. Financial institutions are using Ripple to underpin low-value remittance products for consumers and real-time cross-border payments for corporations and small to medium-sized businesses.

The Ripple solution
Ripple enables financial institutions to make cross-border payments in five to ten seconds, as opposed to four to five days using today's systems. Ripple provides visibility into fees and delivery times of the payment before the payment is initiated, thereby giving financial institutions the ability to more clearly communicate the terms of the payment to consumers. Further, Ripple offers end-to-end tracking of the payment. None of these features are available in today's system for making cross border payments.[1]

---

[1] Today, a patchwork of large, global financial institutions utilize correspondent relationships to facilitate cross-border transactions for other institutions.

Ripple is a modern payment solution for financial institutions. Unlike Bitcoin, Ripple is designed for payments in fiat (government-issued) currency, which we see continuing to play a central and pivotal role in financial services well into the future. Ripple is distinct and separate from Bitcoin. Ripple is operated by the financial institutions that use the system and other delegated firms, instead of unknown "miners". It uses more efficient and less energy-intensive processes.

Ripple and enterprise use cases of distributed payment tools:

Preserve existing consumer protections
Unlike direct-to-consumer models where consumers assume currency risk and have no recourse if something goes wrong, enterprise use cases eliminate consumer exposure; financial institutions directly use the technology on behalf of the consumer as currently done with payment solutions like ACH and wires. With the enterprise use of these technologies, existing consumer protection rules remain applicable and unaltered, making this a safer application of distributed payment solutions.

Enable enhanced funds traceability and transaction visibility
Cross-border payments today are facilitated through correspondent relationships between large banks. This system provides little transaction visibility for financial institutions and regulators. Fees, counterparties, and transaction paths are opaque at best, complicating payment confirmations, audits and investigations. Today, an originating financial institution would have better tracking and receipt confirmation by sending a box of cash overseas through FedEx than by sending a payment through the banking system.

Ripple gives financial institutions – from community banks up to the largest correspondent banks – the ability to trace payments in real-time. Further, Ripple enables financial institutions to exchange more payment information (e.g., fees, balance validation, and confirmation) before and after settlement – a significant improvement over today's system.

The transparency afforded by Ripple offers the ability to improve transaction monitoring capabilities at a lower cost to the system overall. Unlike the challenge of identifying users within Bitcoin, financial institutions utilizing Ripple have a continuing obligation to "Know Their Customers" and comply with anti-money laundering, counter terrorist financing laws and sanctions screening obligations. Importantly, their customers' personally identifiable information such as account numbers or unique identifiers are not stored on Ripple's ledger.

Reduce systemic risk: no single point of failure
Unlike existing payment systems, Ripple has no central operator. Ripple is jointly operated by the participants in the network and other delegated firms. Through this approach, Ripple eliminates the single point of failure that exists within today's systems.

104

While the failure of a central processor would disrupt the operation of one of today's networks, a large majority of independent financial institutions using Ripple would need to fail in unison for the system to cease operating. This design improves Ripple's operational resiliency and minimizes the risk of a system failure.

2. Public policy should recognize the various use cases of the technology.

The advent of Bitcoin brought attention to digital currencies as tools used directly by consumers to replace fiat (government-issued) currency. Policy makers around the world have responded with regulations or limitations on digital currencies largely to address consumer risks that stem from this approach.

As the technology turned the corner from a direct-to-consumer offering to an enterprise tool, the use case of digital currencies evolved beyond only acting as a consumer-facing tool to replace fiat currency. For instance, Ripple's native asset, XRP, is used by financial institutions as (1) a security mechanism and (2) a liquidity tool.

Security Mechanism
From a security perspective, XRP acts as a "postage stamp" for payments made on Ripple. Financial institutions using Ripple hold a small reserve of XRP. With each payment made through Ripple, a portion of an XRP is destroyed. Under normal payment volume that portion destroyed is roughly one millionth of a cent.

However, if a bad actor were to penetrate a bank's defenses and attempt to overwhelm Ripple with traffic – possibly a denial of service attack – Ripple will automatically increase the XRP cost per transaction. This process will bankrupt the institution of its XRP reserve and freeze its ability to carry out an attack. This security feature protects the Ripple network from attacks and abuse thereby maximizing Ripple's reliability and operational resiliency.

Liquidity Tool
Ripple is designed for payments utilizing fiat (government-issued) currency. Due to the large number of government currencies and counterparties, quoting the conversion between every possible currency pair can be burdensome and especially difficult when dealing with rarely traded currencies. See Figure 1 below.

To make this process more efficient, financial institutions on Ripple can use XRP as a bridge, or common denominator, between fiat currencies. Used in this way, XRP maximizes currency liquidity and geographic reach of payments in an efficient way.

Importantly, use of XRP as a liquidity tool is entirely optional. Financial institutions can freely opt to quote and facilitate payments solely in fiat currencies.

Figure 1: XRP Improves Efficiency as a Bridge Currency

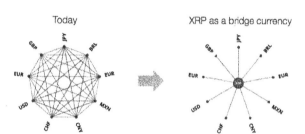

XRP serves operational functions within Ripple and is not designed to be a consumer-facing tool to replace fiat currency. For these reasons we consider XRP a digital asset rather than a currency.

Because of XRP's unique use cases, it carries a different risk profile than a consumer tool like bitcoin or other digital currencies. Ripple urges regulators to recognize the various use cases of the technology and reflect these differences in regulation. We ask policy makers to identify the risks they seek to address and tailor regulations to the tools and use cases that create those specific risks. The regulation that exists in some states today fails to recognize the various use cases and risk profiles of the technology.

While the security mechanism and liquidity tool are alternative use cases that exist today, we firmly believe additional use cases will emerge. Regulation should consider each use case separately. Broad application of one regulatory framework will not effectively identify or mitigate risks. Such an approach will unnecessarily restrain the use of technology and would restrict what would otherwise be a positive innovation in financial services.

In fact, this use case approach is how regulation is written today. Mortgages, swaps, and commodities are all financial assets, but are each regulated differently given their unique uses and risks. We urge policy makers to continue this approach to regulation.

3. A workable regulatory framework is needed to keep the United States competitive.

The current regulatory regime in the United States is highly fragmented, making licensing very cumbersome for start-ups, small companies, and businesses with broad reach. We believe that this fragmentation poses a competitive disadvantage for the United States and undermines our position as a leader in payments.

To keep the United States competitive and a driver of innovation, policy makers should develop a coordinated, national standard for products and services that have national or global reach.

It is imperative that the United States create an environment that supports innovation in a safe and compliant manner. Streamlining balkanized registration requirements via national standards would remove many unnecessary inefficiencies and inconsistencies in our regulatory system.

Other countries have already taken steps to modernize their regulatory and economic policies to support innovation and accommodate these solutions.

For instance, the United Kingdom's Government Office for Science issued a report on blockchain technology, asserting that it, "...provides the framework for government to reduce fraud, corruption, error and...has the potential to redefine the relationship between government and the citizen in terms of data sharing, transparency and trust."[2]

Further, a deputy governor at the Bank of England acknowledged blockchain technologies' security and consumer protection benefits stating, "[t]he emergence of various forms of distributed ledger technology...may reshape the mechanisms for making secured payments."[3] The UK is aware that these technologies are means to a more efficient and prosperous economy.

The United Kingdom's primary regulator, the Financial Conduct Authority ("FCA"), recently launched Project Innovate: an initiative to help start-ups (1) understand the regulatory framework and how it applies to new technology and (2) provide assistance in preparing applications for authorization.[4] The FCA's leadership is creating an environment that supports innovation while ensuring compliance and safety of their financial system.

---

[2] Distributed Ledger Technology: beyond block chain, UK Government Office for Science, January 2016, https://www.gov.uk/government/uploads/system/uploads/attachment_data/file/492972/gs-16-1-distributed-ledger-technology.pdf
[3] "Bank of England to develop blueprint for overhaul of UK payments system," Finextra, 27 January 2016, http://www.finextra.com/news/fullstory.aspx?newsitemid=28391&utm_medium=DailyNewsletter&utm_source=2016-1-28
[4] Financial Conduct Authority, "Project Innovate," http://www.fca.org.uk/firms/firm-types/project-innovate.

Further, Europe has addressed regulatory fragmentation by creating the concept of "passportability." Under this approach, firms that obtain a license to conduct financial services in one European Economic Area are entitled to do business in all other European Economic Areas. Passporting streamlines registration processes and creates a supportive environment for safe, compliant innovation.[5] Investments and future growth for many technology companies is beginning to shift to countries with a more competitive and supportive stance on innovation.

This is in stark contrast to the United States where licenses are needed in nearly every state before a company can begin operating broadly. In light of global efforts to support innovation, the United States must address its fragmented regulatory system if it aims to remain competitive globally. Otherwise, the United States will not be home to future innovation.

4. International coordination is key for effective policy.

While the promise of blockchain technologies is being widely acknowledged, global coordination on how these technologies are implemented and treated by regulators is crucial to ensuring their benefits can be fully realized. Building a consistent, coordinated framework will enable broad adoption of these technologies in safe and prudent ways.

Global coordination has a successful track record of enabling other technology breakthroughs to develop safely. In the early 1990s, the Internet emerged as a promising new tool. Like virtual currencies and blockchain, the Internet offered great potential for economic growth, innovation and inclusion; yet its newness and global scope caused uncertainty and concern about risks.

Policy makers responded to the emergence of the Internet by developing a framework for electronic commerce that recognized the Internet's great potential while balancing its new risks. In 1997, the United States issued a Presidential Directive acknowledging the promise of new technology and setting expectations for safety and risk.[6]

That same year the European Commission followed suit and adopted the Bonn Declaration, a similar framework on global information networks.[7] These frameworks established clear, predictable, and globally-coordinated rules for electronic commerce that ensured security and

[5] Bank of England, Prudential Regulation Authority,
http://www.bankofengland.co.uk/pra/Pages/authorisations/passporting/default.aspx.
[6] The United States White House, Presidential Directive - Electronic Commerce, 1 July 1997
http://clinton4.nara.gov/WH/New/Commerce/directive.html
[7] "European Ministers Adopt Declaration on Global Information Networks, July 1997.
http://merlin.obs.coe.int/iris/1997/8/article1.en.html

privacy. This crucial step recognized the Internet's potential, allowing positive uses of these technologies to take root, and questionable uses to be identified and resolved.

This same approach should be taken with emerging payment technologies today. While we do not know exactly what the future of payments holds, we do know new technology has great potential to improve financial inclusion globally. Yet, without a coordinated regulatory framework, innovation in financial services cannot successfully take root.

In 2015, the Reserve Bank of Australia ("RBA") noted, "[d]igital currencies represent an interesting development in the payments and financial system landscape. The concept of a decentralised ledger is an innovation with potentially broad applications for a modern economy." However, because these technologies are global in scope the RBA stated that regulation should be coordinated globally to effectively identify and address risks. "One vehicle for coordination would be through the Committee on Payments and Market Infrastructure ("CPMI") at the Bank for International Settlements."[8]

The International Monetary Fund stated similar viewpoints in 2016. "The establishment of international standards that take into account the specific features of [virtual currency systems and distributed financial technologies] may promote harmonization in regulation across jurisdictions, and facilitate cooperation and coordination across countries over questions such as the sharing of information and the investigation and prosecution of cross-border offenses."[9]

It is evident that the benefits of these technologies are global in scope. Yet coordinated frameworks play a pivotal role in bringing them to fruition. While it may seem a daunting task, regulatory coordination will ensure risks are effectively identified and managed while the benefits of efficiency, speed, financial inclusion are fully realized. Our legacy of successfully addressing the Internet is promising evidence of our ability to address today's new payment solutions.

---

[8] "Bank for International Settlements cast as digital currency regulator," Finextra, 7 April 2015, http://www.finextra.com/news/fullstory.aspx?newsitemid=27202
[9] "Virtual Currencies and Beyond: Initial Considerations" International Monetary Fund, January 2016, http://www.imf.org/external/pubs/ft/sdn/2016/sdn1603.pdf

Conclusion

The financial services sector along with many central banks have noted the transformative potential of distributed payment technology. Greater speed, improved transparency, and bolstered resiliency offer great promise for the next generation of payments.

The shift from a direct-to-consumer tool within Bitcoin to an enterprise solution within the traditional financial services sector was crucial in leveraging the benefits of the technology while minimizing consumer risk.

For these solutions to take root in the United States, Ripple urges regulators to identify the specific risks they aim to address and acknowledge the various use cases of the tools. Painting all use cases of the technology with one broad regulatory brush will fail to properly mitigate risks.

In light of steps taken in several other countries to support payment innovation, the United States must address its fragmented regulatory regime and licensing requirements if it seeks to remain competitive globally. Ripple urges one standard license within the U.S. and global coordination given the activity enabled by these tools is global in scope.

Distributed payment solutions lay the foundation for an Internet of Value – a network that moves value the same way the Internet moves data. The Internet of Value is a platform on which new innovation, business models, and services can be built. Much like the transformative impact the Internet has had on our lives, the Internet of Value has the potential to transform our financial lives and spur global growth.

[end]